CONSECRATED

One Man's Faith and Courage through
Persecution and Peace, the Holocaust,
and Freedom

DR. ALIX JAROSHEVICH WALSH

Storehouse Media Group, LLC
Jacksonville, Florida

Storehouse Media Group, LLC
Jacksonville, Florida
www.StorehouseMediaGroup.com
publish@StorehouseMediaGroup.com

Ordering Information:

Quantity sales. Special discounts are available with the Publisher at the email address above and type in subject line "Special Sales Department."

Unless otherwise indicated, Bible quotations are taken from the Holy Bible, King James Version.

The views expressed in this work are solely those of the author(s) and do not necessarily reflect the views of the publisher, and the publisher hereby disclaims any responsibility for them.

CONSECRATED: One Man's Faith and Courage through Persecution and Peace, the Holocaust, and Freedom. / Dr. Alix J. Walsh —1st ed.

ISBN: 978-1-943106-26-4 (paperback)
ISBN: 978-1-943106-27-1 (ebook)

Library of Congress Control Number: 2018931408
Printed in the United States of America

CONSECRATED

Dedicated For a sacred purpose. To induct a person into a permanent office with religious rite. Ordained to the office of Bishop. Made or declared sacred. Devoted irrevocably to the worship of God by a solemn ceremony.

–Webster's Ninth New Collegiate Dictionary

Dedication

With love, humility, and gratitude,
I dedicate this book to
God the Father, the Son, and the Holy Spirit.
I thank God for my husband, family, friends,
brothers and sisters in Christ, and all of those being
called from the darkness and into the light.
May God speak to and bless all who read this book.

Epigraph

"We will not hide these truths from our children, but will tell the next generation about the glorious deeds of the Lord, about His power and His mighty wonders.' "So each generation can set its hope anew on God, remembering His glorious miracles and obeying His command" (Psalm 78:4 & 7 NLT).

"Remember your leaders, who spoke the word of God to you. Consider the outcome of their way of life and imitate their faith" (Hebrews 13:7 NIV).

Disclaimer

This book is a true story, written to the best of my ability, based on extensive research, family documents, interviews with people who knew about Konstantin Jaroshevich, and stories my mother had told me.

Acknowledgements

It is with gratitude I wish to acknowledge the following people. Not only have they contributed to bringing this book to reality, they each have, in their own way, been a blessing to me.

My husband Bob, whose love, patience, support, and understanding never wavered as I embarked on this journey.

My sister Ksenia, whom I dearly love. I thank God for our special connection. She has not only contributed to this book, but she has contributed to my spirit.

Pastor John Ferranti, whose gift of prophecy provided confirmation, purpose, and understanding as I stepped into the unknown.

Chaplain Angela Greenway for her friendship, encouragement, gift of discernment, continuous availability to discuss the various pieces of scripture used in this book, and for having the heart of God she so willingly shares with others.

Lois Harris, administrative assistant, and David Hatfield, Executive Director of Polish Christian Ministries, Bel Air, Maryland, for the historical information about Poland and the Churches of Christ and for the work your organization continues. I thank you for being my contact with Mr. And Mrs. Paul Bajko and pray God continues to bless your ministry.

Paul and Adele Bajko, and that although Mr. Bajko has gone to be with the Lord before I had the opportunity to visit him and his wife, I thank them for their ministry, faith, and sacrifice during times of religious persecution in Europe.

Linda Reid, Johnson University, Knoxville, Tennessee, for the information about Konstantin Jaroshevich that was collected by her late husband. Thank you for the lovely conversation and invitation.

Dr. Fabienne Naomi-Smith and Dr. Harold Vick, Jacksonville Theological Seminary, for guidance and knowledge. "My people are destroyed for lack of knowledge" (Hosea 4:6 NKJV).

And to all of the others who have prayed for this book…Thank You.

Table of Contents

Introduction

I began this book to honor the life of Konstantin Jaroshevich and ensure his legacy be carried forward to future generations. He was a man of great faith, courage, and values, attributes that would later sustain him as he and his wife faced formidable persecution.

Not only was his life in jeopardy due to religious persecution, when he witnessed persecution against the Jews and spoke up on their behalf, things became worse for him. Political unrest was the cause of suffering for many people and the enemy of the work he was called to do for the Lord. Unfortunately, persecution, in its many forms, remains alive today.

We should look very closely at what is occurring because as this story reveals, history has a way of repeating itself. It is a reminder to be thankful when we have freedom and peace, something so many do not have yet are willing to die for. We must teach these lessons to our children.

This is a story of man's inhumanity to man as revealed by the Holocaust, as well as the impact of "loving our neighbor as ourselves." This is a story about the choices we make and the courage to make the right choices. This is a story about miracles.

Finally, this is a story about the impact we leave on those we come in contact with and the legacy we leave to the next generation. The results of Konstantin Jaroshevich's work are still evident throughout Poland and parts of Europe.

Konstantin Jaroshevich leaves a legacy of unshakeable faith and love for all humanity.

I pray this story of my grandfather's life will leave you encouraged and blessed.

Chapter 1

A Child Is Born

The late 1800's was a time of extreme poverty and persecution in Eastern Europe. Late one night, surrounded by the darkness and uncertain future, Polusia Jaroshevich, with her husband Michael by her side, began to travail as she brought forth a new life. On September 25, 1891, in Bielsk County, Poland, Russia, she gave birth to a son, whom they named Konstantin.

At the time, that part of Poland was under Russian occupancy, causing their joy to be mixed with fear. The brief exposure to Christianity they had experienced through the Restoration Movement was now forbidden. The state church tried to hold people in ignorance while doctrinal differences among various churches throughout Europe were causing division among believers. However, Michael secretly kept his cherished Bible from those earlier days, often referring to it for peace, strength and hope.

Three days after the birth of his son, Michael placed the baby in the arms of his dying mother, who pleaded with him to give young Konstantin back to God. The New Testament Bible was placed on the head of the newborn child as his father **Consecrated** him to the Lord.

As a young boy, Konstantin worked on his father's farm and attended public school, graduating at the age of fifteen. His interest in the Orthodox and Catholic churches set him on a journey to find the truth. He studied what minimal, often conflicting, information he was able to find.

Because there was no religious freedom in Poland, public discussion of scripture carried severe consequences. Certainly, possession of the Bible could result in expulsion to Siberia. Konstantin knew, however, that "the truth would set him free" and thus continued his search for understanding.

Realizing the impending destabilization of the Slavic countries as well as the increasing danger his son was placing himself in, Michael knew he must do something to save him. Late one evening in April 1910, young Konstantin knelt as again, his father placed the New Testament on his head and repeated the same words he said when he was three days old. Consecrating him again, he placed the Book in his hands.

Then, under the darkness of night, as Konstantin boarded the waiting train to freedom, the old man tearfully cried, "Goodbye son, I'll see you in heaven."[1] So began the journey of Konstantin Jaroshevich to safety and truth.

Chapter 2

Arrival in America

*"I know thy works: Behold I have set
before thee an Open Door, and no man
can shut it. For thou have a little strength,
and has kept my word faithfully, and has
not denied My Holy Name."*

Revelation 3:8 NKJV

In May 1910, the nineteen-year-old arrived in America, the land of freedom, only to have his suitcase stolen. His only remaining possession was the Bible his father placed on his head as he said goodbye.

He found a job in a factory and worked hard to support himself. He worked for two years, earning six dollars a week.

While walking the streets of New York on a hot summer day, he happened upon a meeting at the corner of 1st Street and 2nd Avenue. He was astonished to hear a Christian evangelist, Joseph Keevil, sharing the Word of God. The religious freedom, denied in his homeland, he found on the streets of America. At the end of his talk, Reverend Keevil extended the invitation and young Konstantin went forward, committing his life to the Lord. Soon after, he was baptized, and the ember smoldering so long within him was ignited.

Family Bible in hand, he too began preaching on the streets of the city, as the fire within him continued to grow. He brought the message of the gospel to those on the streets and into the homes of the Slavic people.

During a visit to New York, Dr. Burnham, president of the United Christian Missionary Society, noticed the passion with which the young man shared the gospel. He advised him to continue his education and directed him to Johnson Bible College in Tennessee, assuring him he need not be concerned about money. The English language was enough of a barrier.

"In 1912, with the encouragement of Dr. Burnham and Brother Keevil, Konstantin made the long journey to the Hill."[1]

Konstantin Jaroshevich and John Johnson
New York 1910

At a time when World War I was on the horizon, foreigners were looked on with great suspicion. His

Consecrated

days were long, the language challenging, and the classwork difficult.

Years later, Konstantin wrote:

"While in Johnson Bible College for four years, it was my daily prayer, in the UPPER chamber at 5 in the morning and on the Top-Hill at 5 in the evening; O merciful and gracious Lord God Almighty, let me be Thy humble and faithful servant."[2] And God heard.

In May 1916, Konstantin finished school and was ordained by Dr. Ashley Johnson. He returned to New York and married Ksenia Kostuke, a young woman he met before he attended Johnson Bible College, and together, they became citizens.

The following year, they were blessed by the birth of a son, who they named Alexis. The marriage between Jaroshevich and the woman of God was truly ordained to fulfill **The Great Commission,** in spite of the suffering they would endure.

Although it was their hearts' desires to return to their homeland and share God's love and truth with the Slavic people, the Great War had begun, making such an endeavor too dangerous.

The fire within continued to grow, and he again returned to the streets of New York, taking the gospel to those hungry for the Word of God. He was a well of living waters to the thirsty, and the number of those coming for a drink continued to increase. He organized a Church of Christ on the corner of Clinton and Cherry Streets, continuing to feel the spiritual need of his people, heavy on his heart.

The Jarosheviches moved to Chicago, where they shared the gospel with the Polish people. The ministry continued to grow as he took the message of freedom in Christ from New York to Illinois, and from Ohio to Maryland.

As he continued to go forth with his work of evangelism, "he gathered a score of those able and faithful Christian men and prepared them for ministry service in Poland and Russia,"[3] He knew the tremendous need of a hurting people.

In 1918, Russia withdrew from the war as America's allies advanced. Germany signed the armistice and the war was over, leaving European society destabilized and laying the groundwork for WWII.

Continuing his work, "he established the Evangelical Church of Christ in connection with the American Missionary Society."[4] He was unaware his work was preparing him for a much larger mission field than he could have ever imagined. He waited to hear from the Lord.

In 1919, the Lord called, in the form of a letter from his father. "My dear son, come and lead my people unto our God. See you in Heaven." It was signed, "Your Loving Father, Michael."

Dec. 1920, Rev. and Mrs. Jaroshevich, along with their young son, returned to the village of his birth; 3 days after his father went to eternity.

> *"Go therefore and make disciples of all the nations, baptizing them in the name of the Father and of the Son and of the Holy Spirit, teaching them to observe all things that I have commanded you; and lo, I am with you always, even to the end of the age."*

Matthew 28: 19-20 NKJV

> *"and because thou hast kept My command to persevere, I will also keep thee from the hour of trial, which will come upon the whole world, to test those who dwell upon this earth. Behold, I come quickly; hold fast to what you have; that no man may take thy crown."*

Revelation 3:10-11 NKJV

"The harvest is plenteous but the laborers are few. Pray ye therefore the Lord of the harvest will send forth laborers into His harvest."

Matthew 9:37-38 NKJV

Chapter 3

Return to Poland

"There is a wide-open door for a great work here, although many oppose me."

1 Corinthians 16:9 NLT

"And I saw three unclean spirits like frogs coming out of the mouth of the dragon, out of the mouth of the beast and out of the mouth of the false prophet."

Revelation 16:13 NKJV

It was Christmas Eve 1921 when Mr. and Mrs. Jaroshevich returned to Bielsk County, in the republic of Poland. He was there to begin the work of evangelizing and sharing the gospel with "those who had been held captive to superstition and fear," but he came face-to-face with the horror of lives ruined by the war.[1]

The people, living in spiritual darkness, were faithless, hopeless, and had suffered much. Hunger, misery, and poverty abound. He and his wife experienced strong opposition and terrible circumstances. The people cursed them and made attempts on their lives. "He met with great difficulties and hindrances from the Russian Orthodox and Roman Catholic Priests and also from the government."[2]

The task before them was monumental, but Konstantin knew the truth of God's word would bring personal transformation to the people, eventually influencing homes, societies, governments, and nations, and so he began.

He said, "Before we brought these fifteen million people to the saving and keeping power of the Lord God Almighty, we struggled with the three unclean spirits like frogs to get out of these dear people, for they were, and are, terrible;" as it is written in Revelation 16: 13. He claimed these three spirits were very active in Religion: "1. Making people faithless and religiously confused; 2. Deceiving and dividing people against each other; and 3. Making people ungodly, unrighteous and inhumanly sectarian."[3]

Despite the difficult beginning, their faith remained unshakeable. He shared the gospel with anyone who would listen. He told the people God loved them and

Jesus came to set them free. The message was no longer about purgatory. He offered a suffering people hope.

When God calls, lives change, and God was calling. Slowly, His words began to heal the wounded hearts of the people. Living conditions improved. Stables were built so the animals would no longer be housed with the family. Floors were laid in homes and sanitary condition greatly improved. Children were clean and no longer covered with dirt or flies.[4] The people were taught scripture and some New Testament Bibles were brought into homes. God was moving.

Konstantin traveled by foot from village to village, sharing the "good news." At first, this attracted the curious and the non-trusting, but word about him was spreading quickly, and more came.

"After a year and a half of living among the poorest of Poland, praying for and teaching them, they had their first response." N. Jakoniuk, from the neighboring village of Andrianki, accepted Christ and was baptized."[5]

Dr. Jaroshevich named Jakoniuk minister of the first Church of Christ established in Poland. Soon after, there were more baptisms. It became evident, the cry of the people to hear Jaroshevich was growing at an explosive rate. Wherever he went, hundreds came forward to receive the gift of salvation through Christ. Brother

Jaroshevich would then lead them to the nearest river or lake and baptize them.

The newly converted believers begged for Bibles, but there were none to give. Crowds would gather together in the homes of families that had Bibles and spend many hours studying scripture. They continued to grow in knowledge and faith.

Crowds gathering to hear the Word of God

Konstantin taught the New Testament with simplicity and the spirit of Christ. It was very much like the early Church, as described in the book of Acts. The lessons of faith, love, compassion for the poor and

God's promises and miracles were drawing thousands. The church grew daily.

Konstantin felt blessed that the Lord was using him for such a time as this. Yet he realized the sheep the Lord had given him were mere lambs who needed more care and attention than he alone could provide. In addition, calls were coming for him from all over the country and beyond.

His mission field was mushrooming beyond his greatest anticipation. He needed good, godly helpers to provide care to the ever-increasing flock. Once again, he turned to the Lord in prayer asking for help. The Lord heard him. It was not long after, the answer came.

"Stand fast therefore in the liberty by which Christ has made us free, and do not be entangled again with a yoke of bondage."

Galatians 5:1 NKJV

"Nor is there salvation in any other, for there is no other name under heaven given among men by which we must be saved."

Acts 4:12 NKJV

"The Lord added to the church daily those who were being saved.'

Acts 2:47a NKJV

"Many are called, but few are chosen."

Matthew 20:16b NKJV

"Whom shall I send and who will go for Us?"

Isaiah 6:8a NKJV

"And with many other words he testified and exhorted them saying, "Be saved from this perverse generation." Than those who gladly received his word were baptized; and that day about three thousand souls were added to them."

Acts 2:40-41 NKJV

Chapter 4

God Sends Help

The year was 1924, and Rev. and Mrs. Jaroshevich moved from his hometown to Kobryn, where he planned to establish a mission field office, knowing God would send help. Where would the money come from to pay for such an endeavor? The answer was simple. He sold the farm he inherited from his father, and the money went to meet the expense of his father's dying request: "lead my people unto our God."

First, God sent Bro. Jan Bukowicz from Christian colleges in the United States to Kobryn where he joined Bro. Jaroshevich in his work. Next, He called Bro. Jerzy Sacewicz, who abandoned his training for the Russian Orthodox priesthood, in order to join Jaroshevich.

With this anointed help, the work progressed expeditiously. The number of churches increased dramatically and Bible studies were regularly held in homes. By 1926, there were approximately thirty churches with new ones being added daily. The Mission Head office began to register the congregations, and in 1928, it officially became the Union of the Churches of Christ of Evangelical Confession. "The registration (incorporation) through the provincial office, was important because the government now gave legal rights to the churches."[1]

"Because the people who became Christians came from the orthodox background, the registration had to be done in accordance with the standing regulations of the former Russian Empire."[2]

"The spiritual leadership of the Church of Christ rested on the shoulders of Konstantin Jaroshevich with Rev. Jerzey Sacewicz and Jan Bukowicz handling the administrative and educational affairs."[3]

An orphanage was established in 1928, numerous youth groups formed, and training began for Sunday school teachers. Bible courses were offered and prayer houses built. Jaroshevich began publishing the "Christian Union Regional Monthly."

The growth continued and God's word was spread throughout Poland and its neighbors. The Churches of Christ were established in Russia, Latvia, Romania and other surrounding countries. The people were united with love, joy and the Holy Spirit.

New congregations continued to be formed wherever Dr. Jaroshevich shared his message. Again, more help was needed. "In view of these facts, Dr. Jaroshevich calls upon those men and women he prepared during his five-year ministry in The United States, and upon others he found that were able and reliable."[4] Again, help came.

Konstantin understood the importance of developing and maintaining spiritual unity among the ever-increasing numbers. The training of new ministers, increased missionary outreach, homes for the poor and other charitable activities required coordination. It was time for a transformation of the organization, as it was currently known. This would be a huge undertaking. But, how does one accomplish such a task? What would be the turning point?

"So when they heard that, they raised their voice to God with one accord and said; Lord you are our God, who made heaven and earth and the sea, and all that is in them."

Acts 4:24 NKJV

Chapter 5

A Turning Point

*"Therefore exhort first of all that
supplications, prayers, intercessions and
giving of thanks be made for all men, for
kings who are in authority, that we may
lead a quiet and peaceable life in all
godliness and reverence."*

1 Timothy 2:1-2 NKJV

The turning point for all activities came in 1929, in the
city of Kobryn. Konstantin Jaroshevich called for the
First National Convention of the Churches of Christ, and
the transformation began. Representatives from the
numerous churches attended and a constitution was
adopted, becoming the governing power of the organized
Churches of Christ.

A Board was chosen with Jaroshevich as chairman and the first two helpers God sent, Jerzey Sacewicz and Jan Bukowicz, who served as treasurer and secretary. An executive committee was created with additional members being added as the work of the church continued to develop and expand. The spiritual unity Jaroshevich sought was being accomplished. The churches came together as one, growing still stronger.

The progressive consolidation of the Churches of Christ afforded further development of educational and cultural programs, while guarding the purity of the teachings. Many Bible classes were added, along with the editing of religious literature. Music, under the direction of Bazyli Bajko, became a large part of the ministry. The need for more trained musical conductors became evident. "Young people were being trained to lead youth groups and work at mission stations."[1]

The first convention was such a success, and they became an annual event. People traveled from miles around by whatever means available to attend the spiritually uplifting and educational gatherings. The joy of the people singing resounded throughout the area. Concluding the convention, hundreds, then thousands, would be baptized.

The second convention, in 1930, was held in Horyczow, Wolyn, drawing even larger crowds. Many attending hoped to receive Bibles, but there were just not enough to give. "Brother Jaroshevich gave all he had but the means must be provided to meet the needs."[2] Many Bibles and financial help were needed to ensure all had the Word of God. That same year, "The leaders of the Union of the Churches of Christ took part in the World Convention of Churches, in Washington D.C., and later in Lancaster, England in 1935."[3]

The government of God releases influence and the higher authorities took great interest in the work of the church and Brother Jaroshevich. They, and their activities, were being carefully observed. By the time the third convention was held in 1931, the local government, watching their country being transformed, delegated an official to the religion department of Polesie State; Wladyslaw Kilodziej.

The continuing growth and increasing strength of the Churches of Christ caught the interest of churches abroad. From England to Australia, from the United States to Bulgaria, representatives were being sent to the national conventions to observe and learn the secret of such success. However, there were still not enough Bibles, and the tremendous needs and desires of the people for more were not met.

At the third convention in 1931 it was decided that Brother Jaroshevich would go, as the official representative of the Churches of Christ, to America. He would establish a Mission Office, and by promoting its works, approach Christian organizations for help. So, after many years of devoted and fruitful work, he and his family returned to the United States.

Their son Alexis was accepted into the New York Military Academy, where in his youth, he was a boxer and lacrosse player. He later graduated as a commissioned officer in the U.S. Army, attaining the rank of Captain and serving in the European Theatre during World War II.

The Jarosheviches were well received in the United States. He received a Doctorate of Divinity degree from Tarkio College in Missouri and was a sought-after speaker. "He turned to anybody who would help get Bibles published for the missions."[4]

American churches were supportive and contributed to his cause, but it was difficult to obtain money from individuals, if he did not have a specific committee supporting him. A group from Pittsburg decided to send Dr. Montgomery and a small delegation to Poland to verify all Dr. Jaroshevich was saying.

Upon returning to Pittsburg, the consensus was that what they encountered was so much more than what Dr. Jaroshevich described, and they elected to form a committee. Once formed, they realized they had no jurisdiction over the work in Europe. All they could do was make a recommendation to others to give help. The financial help was therefore slow in coming, but a good man from Pittsburg gave Dr. Jaroshevich an automobile. He sold the vehicle and used the money to buy 100 bicycles for the missionaries who traveled by foot.

Missionaries preparing to travel using their new bicycles

Dr. Jaroshevich and his wife returned to Poland, bringing what they could, offering prayers and encouragement. He continued to lead annual conventions and conduct mass baptisms while seeking ways to provide Bibles to the thousands in need.

Baptism in Kobryn in river Muchawiec, 1934

He recounts, "In 1934, in Poland, with two Americans, two Russians and two Polish prominent men, we came to see the President of Poland, Mr. Boleslaw Bierut and have prayer together on our knees; and after kissing each other, I gave Mr. President the Holy Bible. And Mr. President made the will have Polish Bible published in Poland for Poland and it was done."[5]

Back in America, in 1935, his work continued as he sought additional funding for Bibles and support of foreign missions. He was a sought-after speaker and raised money as he witnessed the struggle for life of those in Poland and surrounding areas.

Through his labors, and those who helped him, the gospel and printed literature reached "Poland, Russia, Yugoslavia, Romania, Bulgaria, Czechoslovakia, and

Hungary."[6] The gospel reached all, from peasants to heads of state, as thousands continued to be baptized.

The brass band leading, thousands to be baptized, during the convention in Poromowo, Wolyn region, 1936

The First World Convention was held in 1936 in England, with Dr. Jaroshevich and Jerzey Sacevich attending. Dr. Jaroshevich, with the help of music director Bazyli Bajko, organized a mission choir to represent them. The choir, complete with full, colorful regional costumes, was a tremendous success.

He then made a way for them to travel to churches in the United States and Canada, giving Christian concerts and spreading much joy. Some were invited to spend the summer in the homes of missionaries or other church families, where they learned to speak English.

It was at this convention that he gave an oration on the Bible as the only way to save ourselves and the

Consecrated

world. He claimed, "The Bible message is practical and timeless, appealing equally to the hearts of man of all races and nationalities and in all periods of history. Thus, the Bible alone can save Russia and the whole world with her."[7]

At the mission office in America, Dr. Jaroshevich continued to raise funds and minister to the Slavic people.

Returning to America, it was agreed by the Union of the Churches of Christ in New York that the Slavic communities here would greatly benefit by bringing eleven missionaries and musical evangelists to the United

States for religious conferences and to minister among the Slavic people. Some in those communities felt called to return to their homeland to help with the work there.

At the end of 1938, the Jarosheviches again returned to Poland, this time, planning for a much longer stay. It was an exciting time.

They arrived in time for the church workers conference "with meetings of the executive committee and mission workers."[8] It was a time of intimacy with each other and the Holy Spirit. They were inspired to build on the Bible classes and, under the leadership of Konstantin Jaroshevich and Jerzy Sacewicz, they were in unity as to the need for a Bible college.

"The work was growing and the many branches required skillful management."[9] The higher level of education would not be spiritual alone, but would help develop strong, well rounded, future leaders.

After asking God for help and blessings, the committee began to act. A plot of land, not far from the Bug River, was identified as the future construction site. Again, God answered their prayer, and funds flowed in as plans were drawn.

"The Jarosheviches attended a tent meeting in 1939. Over 15,000 Christian men and women were there as well as hundreds of missionaries. Hundreds of converts were baptized, and all preparations were made to establish the Bible College."[10]

The most anticipated event of the year was to be the 10th National Convention, held in Zimno, Wolyn, on August 17-20. It was a time of great expectation and excitement as news of the Bible College plans were eagerly received. Thousands of delegates from surrounding countries attended to hear Dr. Jaroshevich, whose work over a span of almost twenty years earned him the respect of all, from peasants to top officials. He was a beacon of hope where none had previously existed.

Dr. Jaroshevich as President of the Union of the Church of Christ

Dr. Jaroshevich was presented with a letter of authority, empowering him, as president of the Union of the Church of Christ, to go abroad, commissioning him to represent and carry on God's work. The document entrusted him with absolute power to execute the affairs of the church.

Dr. Jaroshevich's closing address prophetically told, "Future conventions would be held in reconstructed Poland."[11] He said God's prophecies were being fulfilled.

Who knew the letter he received would provide not only authority, but protection as well?

Who knew their joy would soon turn to sorrow?

THE UNION OF CHURCHS OF CHRIST

OUR MISSION FIELD—FROM THE BALTIC SEA TO THE BLACK SEA—POLAND IS OUR CENTER

OUR CALL
We are called to Preach the Gospel of Christ, to Supply our Polish, Ukrainian, Russian and Hebrew people with Scriptures, to Train and send forth Missionaries, to Pray for their support, to Build up an indigenous Church of Christ and Care for Orphans and the Aged.

HEADQUARTERS
ULICA KOLEJOWA 19,
KOBRYN, POLAND

OUR BELIEF
We believe in the Deity of our Lord Jesus Christ, the Inspiration and Supreme Authority of the Holy Bible, the Blood Atonement, Resurrection and Return of Christ, a Holy and Spirit-filled life, the Unity of God's People and the Divine Mission of the Church of Christ.

EXECUTIVE COMMITTEE

K. J. JAROSZEWICZ, M.A., D.D.
President and General Representative

JAN BUKOWICZ
Vice-President and Treasurer

JERZY SACEWICZ
Administrative Secretary

KONSTANTY SACEWICZ
Missionary Secretary

NIKON JAKONTUK
Missionary Director for Budgetowit State

GREGORES BAJKO
Missionary Director for Polutki State

FEODOR PAWLUK
Missionary Director for Wolunski State

MICHAL SAWIK
Missionary Director for Nowogrolski State

DIMITRY MYSIUK
Missionary Director for Lubliaski State

JAN BUSYL
Missionary Director for Tarnopolski State

MIKOLAJ ZOLUTKO
Missionary Director for Wilneski State

SZYMON BILINSKI
Missionary Director for Lwowski State

JAN WLADYTIUK
Director of Hebrew Missionary Work

BASYL BAJKO
Director of Bible and Music Courses

BORYS WINNIK
Director of Young People's Missionary Work

GREGGORI KASPERSKI
Director of Christian Educational Work

ALEXANDRA WINNIK
Director of Benevolent Missionary Work

TO WHOM IT MAY CONCERN:

This is to certify that by the autority of the TENTH LEGAL CONVENTION OF THE UNION OF CHURCHES OF CHRIST, held in Zimno, Wladimir-Wolynsk, Ukrainia, in the year of our Lord Jesua Christ 193_ August 17-20 and at the session of the EXECUTIVE COMMITTEE, duly elected by the above CONVENTION our dear brother Dr. K.M.J.JAROSZEWICZ (Yaro-she-vich), President of the Union of Churches of Christ is COMMISSIONED to go abroad to carry on the work of Christ and represent the needs of the Union of Churches f Christ before the people of God.

We the CONVENTION OF THE UNION OF HURCHES OF CHRIST place in Dr. K.M.J. JAROSZEWICZ our full confidence and entrst to him the absolute power to execute the affairs of all activities of th MISSION of the Union of Churches of Christ, to organize committees and churces to assist him in his work, to draw affiliation with any sound Evangelical churches and organizations, to disband such committees, sever relationship with such organizations, to accept resignation and to dismiss any individuals wh are unbeneficial to the work of the Union of Churches of Christ and act not n confirmity with him and his policy.

We also empower Dr. K.M.J.Jaroszewicz to act as Treasurer with full power to receive contributions and bequests designated or undesignated and to appropriate them for his work and for th up-building of the Union of Churches of Christ wherever he sees it advisable with full rights to cover his campaign expenses, his office and publicity, his trevelling, his and helper's salaries.

We trust that you will show our dear Representative Dr. K.M.J.Jaroszewicz your kind favor, heartily and prayerfull will cooperate with him, we remain,

Yours in the cause of our Lord Jesus Christ,

The Executive Committee of th Union of Churches of Christ.

Vice-President and Treasurer   Administrative Secretary   Missionary Secretary

White-Russian Missionary Dir.   Ukrainian Missionary Dir.   Russian Missionary Dir.

South Polish Missionary Dir.   Galician Missionary Dir.   Hebrew Missionary Dir.

Polessie Missionary Dir.   Central Polish Missionary Dir.

Rumianian Missionary Dir.   Latvian Missionary Dir.

Bulgarian Missionary Dir.   Estonian Missionary Dir.

Young people's Work Dir.   Bible & Music Courses Dir.

Letter of Authority presented to Konstantin Jaroshevich in 1939

"for equipping the saints for the work of ministry, for the edifying of the body of Christ, till we all come to the unity of the faith and the knowledge off the Son of God, to a perfect man, to the measure of the statue of the fullness of Christ."

Ephesians 4:12-13 NKJV

"Therefore I exhort first of all that supplications, prayers, intercessions and giving thanks be made for all men for kings and all who are in authority, that we may lead a quiet ad peaceable life in all godliness and reverence."

1 Timothy 2:1-2 NKJV

"A good man, out of the good treasure off his heart brings forth good, and an evil man, out of the evil treasures of his heart, brings forth evil. For out of the abundance of his heart, his mouth speaks."

Luke 6-45 NKJV

"And you will hear of wars and rumors of wars. See that you are not troubled; for all these things must come to pass but the end is not yet. For nation will rise against nation and kingdom against kingdom. And there will be famines,

pestilences and earthquakes in various places. All these things are the beginning of sorrows."

Matthew 24:6-8 NKJV

"For when they say "peace and safety!" then sudden destruction comes upon them, as labor pains upon a pregnant woman. And there is no escape.

1 Thessalonians 5:3 NKJV

"Then the Lord reached out and touched my mouth and said, Look, I have put my words in your mouth! Today I appoint you to stand up against nations and Kingdoms."

Jeremiah 1(-10) NLT

Consecrated

Chapter 6

A Time of Sorrow

*"What is causing the quarrels and fights
among you? Don't they come from the
evil desires at war within you? You want
what you don't have so you scheme and
kill to get it. You are jealous of what
others have, but you can't get it, so you
fight and wage war to take it from the.
But, you don't have what you want
because you don't ask God for it."*

James 4:1-2 NLT

Sorrow was on their doorstop, waiting to produce the horror only war can. "On September 1, 1939, Hitler invaded Poland from the west. Two days later, France and Britain declared war on Germany, beginning WWII."[1] Poland was thrown into chaos. Young Paul Bajko, son of Bazyli Bajko, remembered in October

1939, his father sending him to the Union headquarters with two suitcases of food and returning back with the suitcases filled with Bibles.

Not only was it the goal of Hitler to eliminate the Jews, it was also to become a time of great religious persecution. Vast numbers of ministers and missionaries would suffer bitterly.

Dr. Jaroshevich recalled a time in the 1920's, when men of religion were persecuted in Russia. He was riding a train when a group of young officers questioned him. He realized the severity of his situation and responded the only way he knew how. With piercing eyes and a gentle spirit, he calmly and fearlessly began to tell them about God. Their reactions ranged from anger to laughter and they dismissed him, except for the one who continued to interrogate him furiously, eventually becoming more conversational as the hours passed.

"When young Konstantin got off his train, the officer got off with him. They talked all night, and in the morning, the atheist asked for a Bible."[2] So often, it seemed those he brought to God, were people of political and military authority.

Although that meeting ended well, it was now 1939, and he had the distinct feeling, much suffering was to come, and it did. Would history repeat itself?

Dr. Jaroshevich, again prophetically speaking, had his associates sell their Church of Christ building in Brest-Litovsk for cash. They thought he must be losing his mind. What was he thinking? As soon as this was done, he had them purchase fish in tins and bury it an accessible place. He had an urgency about him they did not understand.

On September 17, Soviet troops invaded Poland from the east. Under attack from both sides, Poland fell quickly. By early 1940, Germany and the Soviet Union had divided control over the nation. Panic had taken over the once peaceful nation. Homes were destroyed, families were scattered. The air was heavy with despair and uncertainty.

Thousands streamed into the Union of the Churches of Christ and refugees were pouring in from all directions. The men dug up the food they had buried and watered it down. They shared what they could, but it was not enough and did not last long.

With the country in turmoil, the government turned to Konstantin Jaroshevich, seeking his wisdom and guidance. "The Prime Minister and President knew the influence he had with the people. They ordered him to equip himself with a uniform and report to take charge of the Army."[3]

What was left of the Army was scattered and disorganized. Dr. Jaroshevich had been given an impossible task under the circumstances. The officials fled for their own safety, leaving him in charge of Poland and its people. He held tightly to his New Testament Bible and letter of authority.

He was "ordered to appear before a Russian Commissar named Ilin." He was immediately recognized by the Commissar who said, "I know you. You are the man who has led over half a million of my people to your God."[4] Dr. Jaroshevich witnessed to him and after some time, was released to return to his people.

The people lived in terrible fear. They were starving and being killed. Women and children were deliberately being run over by military vehicles and somehow, amidst all the confusion, Dr. and Mrs. Jaroshevich were separated.

Everywhere he went, people begged him to save them, but he could not. He could not find his wife. Was she alright? He had to go for help.

In his colonel's uniform, he set out on foot toward Moscow. Russian winters are known for their bitter cold, and he was thankful for the colonel's boots that offered him some protection from the elements. "Whenever he could, he would hang on to a passing vehicle, giving his weary feet and legs a rest."[5]

He finally arrived in Moscow. After producing the letter of authority, he was given a meeting with Stalin. Although the meeting went well, no help was available. No one knew where his wife was. Where else could he turn? Turning again to God, he knew he had to try to return to America, to seek relief for his people.

He made his way back to Poland only to find his church with a few starving people remaining inside. Death was everywhere. There was still no sign of Mrs. Jaroshevich. Refugees were being transported in freight cars, to internment or death camps, often arriving frozen. He kept walking, trying to find a way to freedom and help. Everywhere he looked, he witnessed German brutality on innocent people.

He saw a Jewish family, with small children, being mistreated. He could not remain silent. As he watched them being shoved into a pen of swine, Dr. Jaroshevich could no longer suppress his righteous anger and he confronted the officers. Why are you treating them like this? They are children of God. We are to love one another.

The Germans were livid, but so surprised by the boldness of this man, they could not do or say anything, so he kept walking. However, they were soon to meet again; the German brute and the bold man of God.

It was not long before he heard a truck approaching him from behind. As it stopped next to him, the brute leaned out of the window, demanding to see his papers. Without looking at them, he was jerked up and thrown into the truck. After driving through the bitter cold and darkness of night, they arrived at Biala Podlaska, a well-known "death house reserved for political prisoners, religious leaders" and those of various professions.[6]

Dr. Jaroshevich knew of these places. Once admitted, people were never seen again. They either died or were executed. Between the daily beatings and starvation, no one lasted more than a few days. The anguished cries of the prisoners, the stench of death, and the freezing temperatures beckoning them to the dangerous sleep permeated the environment.

Still in his colonel's uniform, Dr. Jaroshevich was thrown into a small room with about twenty-five other prisoners, one of whom was already dead. Several more were not expected to make it till morning. Their bodies would be dragged out and new prisoners thrown in. The cycle of sorrow would then repeat itself.

But in this environment of hate and brutality, something changed. Every morning, when the door was opened, the prisoners looked into the eyes of cruelty as the Gestapo officer came to beat them. He would kick those on the floor to see if they were dead.

The prisoners told Dr. Jaroshevich he would not be able to live under these conditions for much more than a week. As the guards stood outside the door, listening, he began to talk to those in captivity with him. He recited passages from the Bible. To many, those words were like nothing they had heard before. Who was that God that loved them so much? They wanted to know more.

Many of those who were still alive gradually accepted the Lord. The guards continued to listen, and men continued to die. But there seemed to be a light in that dark, cold room and a sense of peace. It was a peace that passed human understanding. Occasionally, scraps of food would mysteriously be "thrown in on the floor, but the prisoners fell upon it and ate, weeping with gratitude."[7] It was as though someone knew Dr. Jaroshevich was in there.

New men were brought in, and Dr. Jaroshevich continued to pray with them. The atmosphere changed in the presence of great faith. After two weeks, all the men in the room when Dr. Jaroshevich arrived had died, and new ones were brought in, yet he remained alive. How could this be? The guards kept listening and observing, as he would tell the men of the glory awaiting them.

He continued to pray and teach them.

The days passed; thirty, then forty, and the daily beatings and freezing temperatures left him stooped over, with legs so swollen he could hardly walk. He was weak, yet continued to pray for the men.

Every morning the Gestapo officer would expect to find Dr. Jaroshevich dead, but each day he remained alive became a personal affront to the position and reputation of the evil German. His anger boiled up within him and the guards became afraid of the brutal officer and apparent unseen, higher authority over the little man of prayer. The situation continued to increase in intensity; uncontrolled anger was face-to-face with the peace of God.

Now, more than fifty days had passed; days of praying and sharing the Word of God. Days the guards listened intently, searching for the source of Dr. Jaroshevich's strength.

Many of them came to believe in the truth, spoken by the man of faith.

On the fifty-third day, the brutal officer again made his morning rounds. Seeing Dr. Jaroshevich still praying brought his anger to the boiling point. Eyes blazing and voice thundering, he pointed to the frail man of God, yelling, "Tomorrow at five, my fine doctor, you will be shot. I have had enough of you."[8]

The guards trembled, and the terrified prisoners prayed all day and into the night. Dr. Jaroshevich told them the story of Peter, in Acts 12, who was imprisoned, under heavy guard and bound in chains, waiting to be put to death. During the night, an angel of the Lord appeared to Peter and a light shone in the prison. The angel woke Peter, saying, "Arise quickly." As he did, the chains fell off and the prison doors and gate of the city opened as he approached, making his way to freedom.

The next morning, they waited and talked about God. The morning came and went. Where was the Gestapo guard who would take him to either be shot by the firing squad or placed in the ovens? The hours continued to pass. No sounds of boots or doors slamming shut. The silence was eerie.

It turned dark, and still no sign of the German brute. Hours passed. Where was he? Did the guards wonder the same thing? What would happen next?

Then, off in the distance, came the dreaded sound of boots on the cold stone floors, coming closer. Holding their breath, they heard the key slowly turning in the old, heavy lock. The door slowly creaked open as unfamiliar soldiers stared into the room. The prisoners were terrified, but Dr. Jaroshevich remained undaunted. The silence was surreal. The prisoners were almost afraid to breathe for fear disrupting the atmosphere.

An older, white-haired man seemed to be in charge. The moments were silent and tense, as his gaze intensely focused on each one in the room. Finally, pointing to Dr. Jaroshevich, he whispered," Who is that man?"[9] No one spoke. Dr. Jaroshevich stood silent, his face lifted toward heaven.

With a burst of emotion, the guard, who had been most intent watching and listening to the humble man of God, cried out to the white-haired man. He begged him to allow him to care for Dr. Jaroshevich.

The white-haired man made no response as he left the cell.

The love and peace of God reached out of the death cell and into the heart of that guard. The prayers had exchanged evil for good. Just as God saved Peter, He would now save his faithful servant.

As doctors were sent in to care for the wounds inflicted by human cruelty, God was present to heal hearts and spirits. Dr. Jaroshevich was given milk, but like Jesus turned water into wine, when "he poured his milk into the tea given to the prisoners, it all became milk."[10] To some, that may have been a surprise, but not to Dr. Jaroshevich. It was God's provision. Simple food was delivered for all.

The following morning, he was taken to the office of the white-haired officer for questioning. Rather than interrogate him, the white-haired man mumbled a few words and made some notations into his record. Dr. Jaroshevich, almost crippled by now, was placed in a separate cell "for observation." The guards, who had observed him for so long, not only continued to watch, they prepared to help him.

The next day, he was again taken to the Commander's office. This time, his wife was waiting for him. The treatment had been so harsh, they barely recognized each other. He was given back his papers, including the letter of authority.

The white-haired officer looked squarely into the eyes of Dr. Jaroshevich and said, "You are free. Take your wife and go."[11]

Who was this man? His spirit was so gentle compared to the German brute. How did he come to be in charge just hours before Dr. Jaroshevich was to be put to death? Could he have been the officer on the train who accepted Christ? Was he an angel or someone whose life was changed years ago because of the ministry of Dr.

Jaroshevich? One may never know that answer, but Dr. Jaroshevich knew God would never leave him. He was a God of miracles and love, able to move people and change situations in the blink of an eye—and He did.

As they left, the guards brought him clothes, some simple food and directions to the train station, making his escape to freedom as safe as possible. The guards watched with thankfulness and respect, as the man who impacted their lives, and his wife, set forth on foot through the bitter cold air. Somehow, they knew he would be safe.

"But beware of men, for they will deliver
you up to councils and scourge you in
their synagogues.
You will be brought before governors and
kings for my sake, as a testimony to them
and to the gentiles.
But when they deliver you up, do not
worry about how or what you should
speak, for it will be given to you in that
hour what to speak.
For it is not you who speak, but the spirit
of the Father who speaks in you."

Matthew 10:17-20 NKJV

"For He Himself has said, "I will never leave you nor forsake you." So we may boldly say, "The Lord is my helper, I will not fear. What can man do to me?"

Hebrews 13: 5-6 NKJV

"What we suffer now is nothing compared to the glory He will reveal to us later."

Romans 8:18 NLT

"Rejoice always. Pray without ceasing. In everything give thanks, for this is the will of God in Christ Jesus for you."

1 Thessalonians 5:16-18 NKJV

"But those who trust I the Lord will find new strength. They will soar high on wings like eagles. They will run and not grow weary. They will walk and not faint.

Isiah 40: 31 NLT

Chapter 7

The Journey to Freedom

*"He shall call upon me and I will answer
him; I will be with him in trouble; I will
deliver him and honor him."*

Psalm 91:15 NKJV

Although the guards provided what they could, the journey to freedom was going to be dangerous, if not impossible. Dr. Jaroshevich had been in the death house with 600 other people. After fifty-three days, only seven remained alive. He was one of them, the only one to walk out alive. God had brought them this far and, despite the difficult journey ahead, he would stand firm on the promises of God.

Once outside the constraints of Biala Podlaska, Konstantin and Ksenia knelt in prayer, thanking God for their release and for each other. Cold, hungry and bearing the physical results of starvation and brutal treatment, they began the five-mile walk, through heavy snow, toward the train station.

It was 1940, an extremely frigid winter and the beginning of compulsory deportation. "Many believers, including presbyters, were sent to Siberia, Kazakhstan or the Ural Mountains. The majority of them never returned, but the Lord gave them the opportunity to witness to others about Christ."[1]

The church was closed down, and people were forbidden to gather and speak in Polish. All discussions were to be in German. The eyes of evil were constantly on the people, watching, listening.

Many risked their lives by holding secret meetings and praying in the Polish language. There was no freedom under "the Russian or German occupation. After a while, all schools were closed down."[2]

The arrests of believers and those not part of the occupation increased dramatically. Hundreds were transported to forced labor camps in Germany as guerrilla war began. Hundreds of people were trying to escape to freedom by any method imaginable. Everyone was under suspicion. Everyone was the enemy. The air was filled with fear. All were questioned. The dangers of their journey were apparent. It was a matter of life or death.

Once they had the train station in sight, they realized the line of those waiting to board was over two blocks long, and people were in lines waiting to see the Governor. The Jarosheviches were in no condition to wait in that long line. Dr. Jaroshevich took his wife and, still in the filthy and well-worn colonel's uniform, they pressed their way to the door, directly in the path of a German guard. Thinking quickly, Jaroshevich said, "Heil Hitler!"[3] The guard opened the door and they went in and briefly saw the governor.

Konstantin said they had plans to go to America, but needed an official paper permitting their departure. He showed him the letter of authorization presented to him at the tenth convention.

The governor quickly wrote a note but asked Dr. Jaroshevich his age. When he replied that he was sixty, the governor said, "You belong to the army. You have to see the Commander of the Gestapo."[4]

Would he let them go? They had eaten what little they had, but the hard journey had taken a further toll on their already fragile condition. What would Dr. Jaroshevich say to the Gestapo Commander? Would he be sent back

Consecrated

to the death camp? How could he survive a second time? His mind was racing.

The Commander was talking to someone as Dr. Jaroshevich approached, paper in hand. He glared at Dr. Jaroshevich, his wife by his side, demanding, "What do you want?"[5]

Handing him the paper, he asked, "Please, would you sign it?" The man talking with the Commander looked impatient. It was apparent he resented the interruption. The commander snatched the paper and threw it on the floor and continued his conversation. Dr. Jaroshevich quietly picked it up and again handed it to him. The commander, without looking at what it was, signed it and threw it to the floor again. Dr. Jaroshevich picked it up, and as they walked away, said "Ksenia, we have permission to leave."[6]

They left quietly, trying not to draw attention to themselves. They had permission to go, and the train was to leave at 10:00 p.m. The time came but no train. An hour later, still no train. They walked to the second station only to find it demolished. There was no sign of a train. Dead and dying bodies were everywhere. The few remaining at that station appeared to be in a state of shock. No one moved. The survivors just stood still, staring. They returned to the first station.

Finally, at 1:00 a.m. came the announcement. Train arriving at first station. The train was only for officers and the military. Anyone else trying to board would be shot on the spot. People were desperate to escape. Panic and fear were everywhere. Now what would they do? They had to get on that train.

They bravely went and stood by the door of the train, along with the police and those examining papers and special tickets. He put Ksenia in front of himself, between the door and the officers. There was much confusion. People were yelling and shoving. Someone was shot.

An officer glanced at Dr. Jaroshevich. He stood as straight as he could, considering his condition, and again, boldly declared, "Heil Hitler!"[7] As soon as the officer turned, he pushed Ksenia on the platform and they entered the train. Somehow, someone "overlooked" checking their papers. How did that happen? Deep within himself, Dr. Jaroshevich knew.

The train was filled with much activity, confusion and noise. Yelling and screaming could clearly be heard from the outside. The car they entered consisted of many small compartments and the sound of doors opening and being slammed shut, seemed almost constant. They found a small, empty compartment with four chairs. They quietly went in, closed the door, sat down and prayed. The train began to move. More shots.

Suddenly, the door opened and two Jewish men were pushed into the cubicle. They had obviously been beaten. Swollen, bruised and with blood on their clothes, Dr. Jaroshevich began to question them. Terror gripped them as they explained they were running for their lives and took the sign off the window, reserving the train for officers and military only. That meant certain death for the Jews. What could he do? Then he asked if they had anything.

Starting to sob, they explained they only had a little bottle of whiskey, but did not drink any of it. They used whisky in the bitter cold weather. Although he never drank, Dr. Jaroshevich insisted they give it to him, knowing if the guards found it, they would make things worse for the Jews. Trembling, they handed Dr. Jaroshevich the bottle.

Again, the door opened, and the two Jews were taken out. With the train still moving, two shots were heard. They knew what had just happened, and again they prayed. Some time passed, and again, the door opened. There stood the conductor and the police.

"Who are you? You have to come here." The Jarosheviches didn't say a word. "SPEAK!" yelled the officer.

Dr. Jaroshevich once more, boldly declared, "Heil Hitler!" "Sir it is so cold. Very cold. I had a little drink."[8] They looked at him, the whiskey bottle and his disheveled appearance.

"All right, all right," said the conductor. "We'll take that," said the officer."[9] They closed the door and placed a sign forbidding anyone to come into the room. They rode all day and into the night, undisturbed.

In the early morning hours, the train appeared to slow down. When it finally stopped, Dr. Jaroshevich noticed another train had also stopped. He asked about it and was told the other train was on its way to Italy. That is exactly what they needed. As the conductor came by, speaking in Czechoslovakian. Dr. Jaroshevich, approaching him, explained he and his wife needed to go to Italy.

The conductor asked what languages Dr. Jaroshevich spoke. He replied Russian, Polish, and English. Hearing that, the conductor instructed them to not come out until he came to get them. And again, they waited.

The conductor returned, showing them how to get on the other train by avoiding examination. He explained, not only do they examine pockets, but a great number of people swallow diamonds and gold coins. He led them to a compound where American men sat, waiting to take the American ambassador.

"Who are you?"[10] they questioned. After examining their passports, they gave them something to eat and a place to wash themselves. They stayed overnight.

"In the morning, they went to see the captain. Waiting there was an American boat." Dr. Jaroshevich explained that they had to go to America on that boat.

"I'm sorry, there is no room, even on the top of the deck. We have only one room, and that is for our ambassador." explained the captain.[11]

Dr. Jaroshevich said, "Captain, our ambassador is in jail. He'll never come out alive. He is condemned."[12]

"What is your name?" asked the captain. After showing him their passports and the letter of authority, he said, "Oh yeah, I have $75.00 for you that somebody sent from America. I'll give you that room." Who sent that money? They never did find out. But God knows.

"Only the intervention of God on their behalf permitted them to make the journey" from Warsaw,

Poland, "across Czechoslovakia and Austria to arrive finally in Genoa, Italy."[13]

Arriving in America, they completed their Journey to Freedom.

"No evil will conquer you; no plague will come near your home. For He will order his angels to protect you wherever you go."
Psalm 91:10-11 NLT

Chapter 8

Home to America

"Every kingdom divided against itself is brought to desolation, and every city or house divided against itself will not stand."

Matthew 12:25 NKJV

The Jarosheviches returned to America in the 1940's. But home is where the heart is, and their hearts were hurting for the Polish people they loved and were led to Christ. They anguished over all those persecuted in the European countries, submerged in the unspeakable consequences of war. They realized how blessed they were to escape just in time.

On April 9, 1940, after Germany occupied Denmark and invaded Norway, WWII began in earnest. Germany invaded France and began extensive bombing of Britain.

"The Royal Airforce (RAF) eventually defeated the Luftwaffe (German Airforce), in the Battle of Britain, and Hitler postponed his plans to invade."[1] Although the United States was not directly involved in the war, crucial aid was provided to Britain.

However, Germany assiduously continued its quest for the "Lebensraum" it needed"[2] for Hitler's Master Race. By overrunning Yugoslavia, Greece and the Balkans, Germany focused its sights on the Soviet Union, its main objective. Man's inhumanity to man reached epic proportions.

The Jarosheviches settled in New York, and the freedom in America afforded Dr. Jaroshevich the opportunity to continue the work of the Lord.

Dr. Jaroshevich, as President of the Churches of Christ, began raising the funds he knew would be needed for the post-war restoration process. He spoke of the struggle for life being endured by the people of Poland, White Russia and the Ukraine. He reminded the American people how much they had to be grateful for and often expressed concern that the blessings of freedom were not fully appreciated. He shared the story of his own personal experiences, his faith and escape to the freedom that many people had died for.

He authored many articles for Christian magazines, encouraging the readers to "Lay up for yourselves treasure in Heaven,"[3] through their donations. He wrote numerous sermons that would later be broadcasted over the radio, thereby reaching thousands of Americans.

His message was simple, true and based on the Laws of God, not man. He encouraged unity among the churches. Without fear of religious persecution, he pushed forward, spreading God's promise of salvation and seeking help for those suffering in war torn Europe.

It was December 2, 1941, the Jarosheviches welcomed the first of three grandchildren into the world. Despite the cold New York weather, the sun shone brightly and America, unlike Europe, was not at war. As the families waited excitedly for mother and child to come home, something happened.

The frightened nurses ran into the rooms, closing the shades and turning off all the lights. Chaos took over as New York went on blackout conditions. It was December 7, and Japanese aircraft had just "attacked the major U.S. Naval Base at Pearl Harbor in Hawaii, taking the Americans completely by surprise and claiming the lives of more than 2,300 troops."[4]

Millions of Americans sat mesmerized as their radios brought the devastating news into their homes. Cities went on blackout conditions and a somber hush fell across America. The next day, President Franklin Roosevelt declared war on Japan, and America changed.

As the nation prepared for battle, the young couple brought their baby home to an uncertain world. Within hours, Dr. Jaroshevich appeared at their apartment. He went straight to the cradle, lifted the infant high above his head, and **consecrated** the newborn to the Lord.

As the parents tried to adjust to the routine of sleepless nights, the nation was adjusting to a new routine as well. "America needed to quickly raise, train, and outfit a vast military force. At the same time, it had to find a way to provide material aid to its hard-pressed allies in Great Britain and the Soviet Union."[5]

Although the country was coming out of the Great Depression of 1929 and the economy was improving, "America was now drawn into a global war."[6] The costs would be staggering, requiring many sacrifices and cooperation on the home front. Many lives of loved ones would be lost.

Dr. Jaroshevich feared what he had spoken so often about, may now be experienced in this land of freedom.

Where there is no unity-there is disaster, so Americans stood united, as ONE NATION UNDER GOD, against the disastrous forces of evil. Churches united as prayers for peace and safety were heard across the land.

Anticipating the threat of war in 1940, President Roosevelt initiated, and Congress approved, the first peacetime draft. By December 1941, when war was declared, there were over two million members in the military. By 1942, over ten million civil defense volunteers.

The Jarosheviches' son was a member of the 101st Airborne and served in the European Theatre. Mexican-Americans, African-Americans, Chinese, Japanese, and Native Americans joined together in unison, as Military Brothers.

Filling the gaps in the workforce, six million women combined their efforts to perform jobs previously held by the men. The Women's Auxiliary Army Corp was established, utilizing 350,000 women in non-combat positions.

Rationing, conservation and recycling became a new way of life. Victory gardens were planted by average citizens, producing over a ton of food to help where shortages existed.

The unemployment rate dropped to one percent as the production of goods needed for war changed the face of manufacturing.

Patriotism was worn like a badge and displayed with honor.

On June 6, 1948, as the Normandy invasion was beginning, President Roosevelt, via radio, prayerfully addressed the greatest nation on earth. He began by; "Almighty God: Our sons, pride of our Nation, this day have set upon a mighty endeavor, a struggle to preserve our Republic, our religion, and our civilization, and to set free a suffering humanity. Lead the straight and true; give strength to their arms, stoutness to their hearts, steadfastness in their faith. They will need thy blessings."[7] He further went on to say the "men's souls will be shaken with the violence of war."

Throughout the prayer, President Roosevelt asked for strength and grace for family members and the country as a whole, and pleaded for the faith of this nation to never falter, no matter the circumstance.

He concluded, "With Thy blessing, we shall prevail over the unholy forces of our enemy. Help us to conquer the apostles of greed and racial arrogance. Lead us to the saving of our country, and with our sister Nations into a world of unity that will spell a sure peace, a peace invulnerable to the scheming of unworthy men. And a peace that will let all of men live in the freedom, reaping the just rewards of their honest toil."[8]

From the privacy of their homes, the prayers of a nation were heard.

The following year, President Roosevelt died in office, leaving Harry Truman to continue in his role. The casualties were heavy in Normandy and the following campaigns in Iwo Jima and Okinawa. A land invasion of Japan would mean many more American lives lost. In order to avoid such a tragedy, in early August 1945, President Truman authorized, for the first time, the use of the atomic bomb on Hiroshima and Nagasaki. Japan surrendered on September 2, 1945.

WWII was over, but it left behind a path of devastation. More than fifty million lives were lost, including six million Jews, at the hand of Hitler. Many husbands, sons, fathers, lovers and friends would never return home. The Jarosheviches' son did return, and again they thanked God. The legacy left by the war, was the spread of communism and the cold war between the United States and the Soviet Union.

The continued unity of the American people was displayed, as they reached out to each other, to help and comfort the many hearts that were heavy and to

celebrate with those who made it home. Life tried to
return to normal.

"To everything there is a season,
A time for every purpose under heaven:
A time to be born,
And a time to die;
A time to plant,
And a time to pluck what has
been planted;
A time to kill,
And a time to heal;
A time to break down,
And a time to build up;
A time to weep,
And a time to laugh;
A time to mourn,
And a time to dance;
A time to cast away stones,
And a time to gather stones;

A time to embrace,
And a time to refrain from embracing;
A time to gain,
And a time to lose;
A time to keep,
And a time to throw away;
A time to tear,

And a time to sew;
A time to keep silence,
And a time to speak;
A time to love,
And a time to hate;
A time of war,
And a time of peace;

(Ecclesiastes 3:1-8) NKJV

It was now a time to heal.

Chapter 9

The Healing Begins

*"I have heard your prayers and seen
your tears. I will heal you."*

2 Kings 20:5 NKJV

To Heal: "To make sound or whole; to restore to health; to cause an undesirable condition to be overcome; to mend; to restore to original purity or integrity or return to a sound state."[1]

Healing from the trauma of WWII would take days, months and even years, as combat not only impacts nations and economies, it impacts individual bodies, minds and souls.

The world now tried to adjust to peace.

The Jarosheviches welcomed their son home. Like many families, he was reunited with his young wife while adjusting to the small child he had to leave shortly after birth. It was a time to celebrate. For those who did not return, healing took place through the grieving process, some completing it with more ease than others. For too many however, the battle continued in the form of PTSD, often referred to as "shell shock." Those returning with physical disabilities, missing limbs, and other afflictions also had their own battle ahead of them, often suffering PTSD as well.

As healing began and personal adjustments made, Americans moved forward. No longer was manufacturing focused on the producing the necessities of war; it turned to the things that made homes and lives better. Metals could now be used for cars and household appliances. There was a renewed sense of thankfulness, unity, love and peace. Churches flourished and the baby boom began.

Americans felt blessed the war was not fought on our soil, but Dr. Jaroshevich knew Europe was not so fortunate, and he made preparations to return. Knowing his plans, the Churches of Christ planned a special convention in his honor.

The war changed the borders of Poland dramatically, with different provinces being annexed to the Ukraine,

Belarus and the Soviet Union. 70 of the Churches of Christ remained in the Soviet Union and they joined the "All Russian Evangelical Christian Baptist Union."[2] However, many churches and towns were completely destroyed as the German tanks rolled over Poland. The sewers became the filthy, disease-ridden environment where the Polish military found refuge during the battle.

When Dr. Jaroshevich arrived in Olsztyn in August 1946, he brought what he could in funds and material support. It was here the convention took place, with the primary topic being the post-war situation of the Union. He thought it would be best to resign from his position as chairman of the Union, enabling one of the local, faithful church leaders the opportunity to assume that role. "Jerzy Sacewucz was unanimously chosen as the new chairman and Dr. Jaroshevich accepted the office of honorary chairman and the Union's general council abroad."[3]

In November, the Union of the Churches of Christ in Poland was granted the ability to resume its pre-war activity and was able to function legally and independently.

In 1947, Dr. Jaroshevich again returned to Poland. This time, besides clothes, food, and other supplies, he brought the funds necessary to purchase a bombed-out building in Warsaw. The building would become "the Union's main office and a meeting place for the local congregation."[4] Before returning to America, he provided additional funds for charitable purposes.

His final trip to Poland was August 13-15, 1948, to attend the 12th National Convention in Warsaw. "The convention was marked with the ordination of forty church workers" of newly planted churches.[5] At this convention, Jerzy Sacewicz, his faithful helper for so many years, was married, with Dr. Jaroshevich performing the ceremony. It was a time of healing and rejoicing.

Dr. Jaroshevich returned home to stay. He was recognized for his years of campaigning in America for the Polish people. In 1949, he was awarded the Order of Poland Restored (Polpnia Restituta) by the Polish Ambassador in Washington.

"The same year, he was also consecrated for the Patriarchate of Alexandria by Archbishops Christopher Contogeorge and Arsenios Saltas through the Russian Orthodox Church."[6]

On September 19, 1950, nine days after the 13th annual convention in Warsaw, "Poland fell under the terror of Stalin and his agents."[7] "The Communist minority in the Polish government, with aid from Russia, seized control of the government."[8]

The building of the congregation was seized and use of the chapel was forbidden. Apartments were given to Communists and sympathizers."[9]

"During these difficult times, five small churches, including the Churches of Christ, formed an Evangelical Union as a means of survival."[10] Being accused of cooperating with the west, the arrests of religious leaders, from all churches, began again.

Chapter 10

The Work Continues

"The Spirit of the Lord is upon me,
because He has anointed me to preach
good tidings to the poor; He has sent me
to heal the brokenhearted, to proclaim
liberty to the captives, and the opening of
the prison to those who are bound; to
proclaim the acceptable year of the Lord,
and the day of vengeance of our God; to
comfort all who mourn.
Isaiah 61: 1-2 NKJV

Back in America to stay, Dr. Jaroshevich continued the work of the Lord.

The establishment of the United Evangelical Union in Poland exemplified what could be accomplished when related churches learn the benefits of "cooperation, respect, or diversity on minor issues."[1]

The Union of Churches of Christ joined that effort in 1953 and, although the Union in Poland did not survive past 1987, it survived the demise of many churches during Stalin's reign and produced much good for the people in that area. Their strength was in God and unity.

Like Europe, the need for unity and evangelism was necessary for churches in America to remain strong and free. "Konstantin Jaroshevich was active in building bridges with other Orthodox groups and opposed the narrow and reductive Orthodoxy of many within the church."[2]

Despite some politically inconvenient discussions, he continued his quest to unite churches. This, unfortunately, led to some fractious relationships, but he was focused on the Word of God, not man.

"The challenge to the Western Rite is to sustain the true Orthodoxy handed down from our parents while building an American expression of the ancient faith of true Orthodoxy in such a way as to honor our parents, their faith and traditions."[3] Additionally, the challenge is not only "to build an American expression of the faith that is truly Orthodox, while remaining faithful to the promise that is America."[4]

Religious leaders from the East began to pour into America to escape religious persecution.

After spending time in a forced labor camp, "a young Polish refugee from one of the rural congregations in Eastern Poland, arrived in America as a displaced person."[5] This was the same young man, Paul Bajko, who delivered two suitcases of food to the Church of Christ headquarters in Poland in 1939.

Through the European Evangelistic Society, he was directed to Eastern Christian College for his education and preparation for service to God. Young Paul had spent many hours in the home of the Jarosheviches in Poland and was very familiar with the work of Dr. Jaroshevich in the Church of Christ. Upon completing school, he continued the work of Dr. Jaroshevich and, in 1954, founded The Polish Christian Ministries in Bel Air, Maryland. That ministry is active today.

The need for unity among the various churches fleeing to America was increasing. As Dr. Jaroshevich became involved in the Standing Episcopal Conference, the work continued.

It was a time to build.

Chapter 11

A Time to Build

*"According to the grace of God which is
given to me, as a wise master-builder, I
have laid the foundation, and another will
build on it. But let each take heed how he
builds on it."*

1 Corinthians 3:10 NKJV

The Standing Episcopal Conference of Orthodox Bishops
was the first ecumenical body of Eastern Orthodox
hierarchs in America and was fully established in 1951.
The SEC "predates the Standing Conference of the
Canonical Orthodox Bishops in America, founded in
1960, and the present Assembly of Canonical Orthodox
Bishops in North and Central America, formed in 2010."[1]

The struggle to establish the Orthodox Church in America was the result of religious persecution in the Eastern religious environment. They came to America for the freedom to express their faith and cherish the values this country was founded on. They came, bringing their own religious leaders, to establish their cultural and religious lives here. "Lacking their own church and hierarchy. They began attending Polish and Slovak Rite Roman Catholic churches."[2] Confused and often disillusioned, some associated with other denominations while others lost their faith completely.

This was not a new phenomenon. It was a sacramental movement with its roots going back to the beginning of Christianity. History seems to have a way of repeating itself. With each apostolic succession, new needs of the faithful clearly challenged the early Apostolic Canons. Although the church was focused on the early canons, it acknowledged some adaptions would be necessary and valid to resolve specific situations and circumstances while maintaining its apostolic traditions. The married episcopate is such an example.

To overcome the restrictions on the Eastern churches and cooperate across ethnic boundaries would require careful building.

"To fulfill the urgent needs of Ukrainians in the United States, Archbishop +PALLADIOS (Rudeno) arrived in New York City to take up his responsibilities as ruling bishop; and, in 1921, he established the Holy Ukrainian Autocephalic Orthodox Church in Exile. He had escaped to Greece after the Russian Revolution."[3]

And thus, the foundation was laid, but the building did not progress without facing many obstacles.

Efforts to bring the Orthodox Church together in America, where "warring jurisdictions could find unity and brotherhood,"[4] were often met with pride and rejection. The ethnic bodies placed themselves over orthodoxy, thereby undermining many efforts. The Eastern Churches rejected the young American Church.

However, the builders took great heed in the process. Like the Orthodox Catholic Church in America (OCCNA), many continued as a traditional body without losing the traditions of the early Apostolic Church. "The OCCNA today works to bring jurisdictions together (just as it was originally created to do)."[5]

The effect of two world wars resulted in numerous partitions and annexations in many countries. Boundaries were drawn and redrawn with political and religious authorities often in conflict with each other.

Such was the case of Belarus, dating back to 1795. "After the partition of Poland and the annexation of

Belarus by Russia, in 1795, the religious affiliation of Belarus became divided between The Russian Orthodox Church and the Roman Catholic Church, with a small minority of Greek Orthodox and Protestants."[6]

By 1922, former members of the Polish Orthodox Church founded the Byelorussian Autocephalous Metropolia, but this was suppressed in 1938 during Stalin's "Great Purge." Again, the succession of hierarchy continued through the Nazi regime and, in 1946, was absorbed into the Russian Orthodox Church outside Russia. The conflicts between State and Politics versus True Orthodoxy continued.

Many attempts to break free from relationships with the Roman Catholic Church in Rome and The Russian Church in Moscow were unsuccessful. In 1945, the Patriarch of The Russian Orthodox Church in Moscow issued an Ukase (proclamation) stating, "It would only recognize the Russian Orthodox Church in America if the latter would abstain from political activities against the USSR and effectively cede control of its affairs to Moscow."[7] Agreeing to this, the American Church could well become a KGB base on our home soil. The Ukase would be rejected by the young American Orthodox Church.

Those who left the suppressed churches in the East, came to America, so they could share the Word of God and not have to take the church "underground" to do so. The hierarchs in America worked together, knowing a church divided against itself cannot stand. They came to share the truth. Corrupted men hide the truth and change it for greed or evil.

The young American Orthodox Church was planted to bear good fruit. It would become the tree of life to many.

To further the unity of the Ukrainian jurisdictions in America and promote the true New Testament church, a convention was called, in 1949, to specifically address the current situation and challenges. This was to become, in 1951, the Standing Episcopal Conference.

"The Eastern Orthodox was becoming indigenous to America."[8]

The building of the Free Orthodox Church had not only begun, it was breaking free from the holds of Europe.

The *New York Times* reports the formation of the Standing Episcopal Conference, October 14, 1950.

CHURCH ENDS MOSCOW TIE
Russian Orthodox Communion in U.S. Will Be Independent

SPRINGFIELD, Mass., Oct.13 (AP) The Russian Orthodox Church in America announced today that it was breaking all ties with Moscow and would henceforth function independently of Russia.

Leaders of the church, meeting for the first time on their own initiative, named Metropolitan Bishop Joseph Krimowicz of Springfield as Patriarch of the church in the United States.

Metropolitan Bishop Konstantin Jaroshevich was chosen Patriarch of the church in all foreign countries.

Archbishop Joseph Zielonka of the Old Catholic Church of New Jersey was elevated to Hierarchical Bishop and Bishop Damaskinos of California to Archbishop.

"The first moderator of the Standing Episcopal Conference was Metropolitan Joseph Kimovich of the Russian Orthodox Church in America. Other member hierarchs were Metropolitan Fan S. Noli of the Albanian Orthodox Church, Archbishop Arsenios Saltas, Exarch in the United States of the Greek Orthodox Patriarchate of Alexandria, Metropolitan Nicholas Bohatyretz of the Ukrainian Orthodox Church in Canada, Archbishop

Consecrated

79

Konstantin Jaroshevich of the Alexandrian Patriarchate and admitted by ekonomia-Archbishop Josef Zielonka of the Polish Old Catholic Church of America and Europe. The new bishop Zurawetsky was also a member; he had been consecrated to the Sacred Episcopate at St. Peter and Paul Orthodox Church, Springfield, Mass., on 15 October 1950 by Metropolitan Joseph Kimovich assisted by Archbishops Jaroshevich, Bohaatyretz, Zielonka and Peter M. Williamovicz (of the Polish Old Catholic Church)."[9]

On this, the building would be strong. But, there was still much to do. The 1950's had issues of its own.

"Therefore, brethren, stand fast in the traditions with which you were taught, whether by word or epistle."

2 Thessalonians 2:15 NKJV

"Beware of false prophets, who come to you in sheep's clothing, but inwardly they are ravenous wolves. You will know them by their fruits. Do men gather grapes from thorn bushes or figs from thistles? Even so, every good tree bears good fruit, but a bad tree bears bad fruit...therefore, by their fruits you will know them.

Matthew 7:15-17 NKJV

Consecrated

Chapter 12

The 1950s: A Religious Resurgence

Today, "The Holy Orthodox Catholic Patriarchate of America and Standing Episcopal Conference of Orthodox Bishops are the same entity,"[1] "It has long established criteria, crucial for member hierarchs and jurisdictions belonging to the Standing Episcopal Conference."[2] These criteria ensure adherence to the ethics and morality of the New Testament Church of Jesus Christ, providing unity of the one Holy Catholic and Apostolic Church.

The establishment of the Standing Episcopal Conference in 1951 laid the groundwork to develop further unity while addressing the differences in religion and views of the changing political and social environment.

With each apostolic succession and appointment, the building continued as differing opinions and biblical interpretations were presented. "In 1954, Archbishop Jaroshevich was appointed Exarch of the Greek Orthodox Patriarchate of Alexandria and All Africa in The United States. Archbishop Jaroshevich was **consecrated** to the Sacred Episcopate."[3]

The post war period was a powerful time of religious resurgence, peaking in the late 50's.

"It was a fine time to go to church—and to build. It was a decade when the American Family was embraced as an institution by men and women seeking normalcy after WWII."[4] Church membership increased dramatically, with organized religion shaping U.S. politics and the daily lives of Americans. Women left the labor market, providing jobs for returning veterans, and assumed the role of domesticity.

As marriage and birth rates soared, the increasing national wealth afforded the purchase of new cars and dreamt about homes in the suburbs. "The GI Bill enabled record numbers to finish high school and attend college. This led to increasingly skilled workers and yielded higher incomes for families."[5] As the economy continued to boom, "the things of this world" were more available than ever before.

In 1953, during his first year of presidency, Dwight Eisenhower "decided to get baptized in the Presbyterian Church."[6] Shortly thereafter, the words "Under God" became part of the Pledge of Allegiance, and "In God We Trust" was added to the currency of the United States. A day in school often began with prayer.

The United States was the strongest military power, and according to British Prime Minister Winston Churchill, "stands at the summit of the world." America seemed to "have it all."

The religious resurgence continued, with new churches, offering many options, springing up everywhere. On any given Sunday, half the population could be found attending church. This was the new norm. People had so much to choose from and the churches were anxious to provide what they wanted. It was a spiritual marketplace. Some churches began to relax their rules connected with organized religion so as to please their congregations. Although for some, this was somewhat freeing, for others, it was a wandering from doctrine, causing confusion.

As Archbishop Jaroshevich continued to build bridges, he consecrated numerous bishops and archbishops into orthodox churches, enlarging and unifying apostolic leadership. Continuing his involvement in the SEC, he boldly addressed issues that pertained to the spiritual, political and personal lives of Americans, using the Bible as the ultimate authority. He continued to promote the New Testament Church while fulfilling The Great Commission.

The 1950's also saw the surge of the Evangelical Church. Represented by such powerful leaders as Billy Graham, the trend toward national celebrity ministers, broadcasting via radio and television, was reaching thousands. Mega churches in the suburbs were displacing the small church leaders of fundamentalism.

The manifestation of the Holy Spirit, so often not acknowledged by some denominations, now challenged religiosity. Smith Wigglesworth, who died in 1947, was not only used by God to heal the sick and deliver people from evil spirits, he raised the dead. Kathryn Kuhlman filled auditoriums with people who came to receive and did many healings. Both walked in the spiritual gifts of God, reaffirming such miracles did not stop with the passing of the apostles.

This was an added dimension to the religious resurgence, all contributing to the restlessness of the people. The illusion of normalcy and organized religion was becoming out of focus. Tensions were brewing. The 1950s were becoming "an era of great conflict."[7]

A shift was taking place.

"For the world offers only a craving for physical pleasure, a craving for everything we see, and pride in our achievements and possessions. These are not from the Father, but are of this world. And this world is fading away, along with everything that people crave.

1 John 2:16-17 NLT

"I urge you to offer your bodies as living sacrifices, holy and pleasing to God-this is your spiritual act of worship. Do not conform any longer to the pattern of this world, but be transformed by the renewing of your mind. Then you will be able to test and approve what God's will is-His good, pleasing and perfect will."

Romans 12:1-2 NKJV

But the manifestation of the Spirit is given to each one for the profit of all.
For to one is given the word of wisdom through the Spirit, to another the word of knowledge through the same Spirit, to another faith by the same Spirit, to another gifts of healings by the same Spirit,

Consecrated

to another the workings of miracles, to
another prophecy, to another discerning
of spirits, to another different kinds of
tongues, to another the interpretation
of tongues.
But one and the same Spirit works all
these things, distributing to each one
individually as He wills.

1 Corinthians 12:7-11 NKJV

Chapter 13

The Shift

Despite the Religious resurgence, the shift began to reveal some underlying divisions in society.

The illusion of normalcy, organized religion and family focus no longer appeared to be all satisfying. What was missing? Tensions were brewing. It was becoming a time of conflict. Many women were no longer content with their domestic role and reentered the workforce. "Men of that decade felt deep, almost inexpressible, tension between the postwar nesting instinct and those other restless drives. Expressed in religious, or quasi-religious ways, the alternative impulses helped shape the spiritual underground."[1]

Catholic-Protestant relations became strained. "Conflict between theology and popular faith grew.[2] The role of women in the church was often divisional in the home, as well as in various denominations. Clerical celibacy was challenged by married bishops and remains a topic of discussion today. On March 14, 2017, Pope Francis stated, "We have to think about married priests in the Catholic Church."

Archbishop Jaroshevich spoke boldly about the conflicts between doctrine vs discipline, liberal vs evangelical, and women in ministry. Recognizing the influence women had over their children, he said, "God bless the women who are out and out for Jesus, and God help those who are not, those who are causing many to err."

These sensitive issues were further exacerbated by such things as birth control (the pill), religious intolerance, public funding for parochial schools and discrimination.

Still, Americans had other things on their minds and hearts. The shift was growing. The world was changing.

Pursuing the mandate of *Brown vs Board of Education*, "the integration of schools, in Little Rock, Ark, regardless of race, creed or religion, paved the way for the Civil Rights movement."[3] The segregated face of society was changing.

The fifties brought new fashions, music and entertainment, that seemed to be a variance from the conservatism Americans were known for. The Salk polio vaccine was introduced, saving thousands of children from a life of paralysis. The Soviet Union launched *Sputnik*, and the United States followed by launching *Explorer 1*. And the space age began. The race was on.

The restlessness continued. Although America came through WWII, it did not mean disputes among nations were over. All was not quiet.

It was the atomic age, and the Cold War began between the two super powers, the United States and the Soviet Union. Americans were now involved in a prolonged battle of will, pride, threatening postures and the constant threat of the use of atomic, and subsequently nuclear weapons. The state of geographical tension divided countries as they either sided with the United States and its allies or the Western Bloc.

Any military leader knows, to divide and conquer is the secret to winning the battle. Satan is no exception. He has come to steal, kill and destroy. In her book, *He Came to Set the Captives Free*, Dr. Rebecca Brown explains," Satan knows if he can successfully break up the family unit, he will also break up the unity of the church, and I might add, of our nation." Would the next step put nation against nation?

These tensions and lack of peace, continued to reshape America. The long-term threat of Communism, known as the Cold War, contributed to the restlessness and searching. What would the future hold? The shift had widened. This is a topic Archbishop Jaroshevich spoke of often.

"WHAT SHALL WE DO"

"It has been considered even before the First World War. HOW TO SAVE RUSSIA AND WITH WHAT MEANS OR POWER?

  A. Economical applications have failed.

  B. Political efforts have failed.

  C. Military power has not only failed, but has made Russia stronger and more dangerous.

  D. Is there anything else left now, that Political and Military Leaders, can use to save Russia, and with her, the whole world? What about it?

Now the following questions are before us.

  1. What shall we do?

  2. Have we failed completely?

  3. Are we going to give up and surrender?

  4. Or, shall we use the military power?

5. Are we sure, that by using military power, we will save Russia and ourselves too?

"Since we are living in the Atomic Age, we must understand that our knowhow in using atomic power does not rest entirely in our POSSESSION. In case of using this atomic power, we may know how to start it, but would we be able to stop it?"

The above is part of a speech Archbishop Jaroshevich gave in 1947 at the World Christian Convention. It was his belief that the Word of God was, and is, the most powerful of weapons. By evangelizing to the unsaved part of the world, and providing Bibles, the Great Commission would be filled and there would be peace.

It was not until the 1980s that Ronald Reagan of the United States and Michael Gorbachev of the Soviet Union agreed to replace fear and domination with openness and restructuring. It was a move from division to unity. Another shift was taking place.

Many years have passed since, but are we any safer? Is the world more peaceful? Are our children safer? We now have nuclear weapons, and war still looms. Do we truly understand what kind of war we are fighting? Archbishop Jaroshevich did.

For we do not wrestle against flesh and blood, but against principalities, against powers, against the rulers of the darkness of this age, against spiritual hosts of wickedness in the heavenly places.

Ephesians 6:12 NKJV

As the shifting continued, we must wonder---what was happening? What is the answer?

"Be sober, be vigilant, because your adversary, the devil walks about like a roaring lion, seeking who he may devour."
1 Peter 5:8 NKJV

"Lest Satan should take advantage of us; for we are not ignorant of his devices."
2 Corinthians 2:11 NKJV

"Depart from evil and do good; Seek peace and pursue it. The eyes of the Lord are on the righteous, And His ears are open to their cry."

Psalm 34:14-15 NKJV

Chapter 14

What Was Happening

*"Woe to those who call evil good, and
good evil;
Who put darkness for light, and light
for darkness:
Who put bitter for sweet, and sweet
for bitter!
Woe to those who are "wise in their own
eyes, and prudent in their own sight"*

Isaiah 5:20-21 NKJV

During the late 1950s and into the 1970s, the storms of
life continued to churn. The battle between good and evil
again reared its ugliness, as the cold war, which was an
indirect conflict between the United States and the Soviet
Union, gave way, in 1959, to the Vietnam War.

Although America was not directly involved until 1965, we again sent our young men into combat. The nation clearly recalled WWII and its impact on their lives. That was a time when the nation and families came together, trusting in God.

The Jarosheviches moved to a modest cottage in Virginia Beach to be close to their son and his family. He joined and became active in the Aragona Church of Christ, where he often witnessed to neighbors, shopkeepers, and total strangers.

The explosion of post-war births produced a new generation that would be sent to war. Again, the cycle would be repeated. But this time, something was different.

Although Archbishop Jaroshevich was now in his mid-seventies, He continued writing and remained involved in delivering Gods message wherever he could. He was concerned about the apparent changing values of American society.

The divorce rate was rapidly increasing. The baby boomers developed a suspicious attitude toward the government and adult society in general. Leaders appeared to be seduced by power and money. Values were changing. The Church no longer seemed to meet their needs.

The Vietnam War was also becoming a war between the generations and, unlike the family unity of the 1940s, a widening shift was developing. Many of the generation of baby boomers were no longer willing to accept the middle-class lifestyle and its traditional values. They were often viewed as hypocrisy when compared to what they observed in their homes and communities. This shifting paved the way for the emergence of a counter culture.

As America sent its young men off to war, the most unusual and unexpected social movement began. The hippies appeared and the counterculture began. Unshaven, long haired, hippie men were in direct contradiction to the clean-shaven and short hair requirements of the military. The phrase "make love, not war" became a familiar chant among the exuberant, youthful, social rebels.

They rejected the culture of the middle class as they became engulfed in their personal searches for individualism, authenticity and community. They searched for the simpler things. They searched for the truth. As they "did their own thing," rock music, smoking marijuana, psychedelic drugs and an explosion of easy sex were inclusive. Hippie women bore many children out of wedlock.

Although many of their demonstrations were confrontational, the message they tried to portray was one of anti-war. They often carried signs, sang songs and gave out flowers. Their message from this frustrated generation was peace, a stark contrast to the demonstrations of today. There were no riots, guns or vandalism. The search for community led the hippies to form communes, most of which failed.

When Saigon fell in 1975, the counterculture all but disappeared. However, the beliefs and practices of the counterculture of the 60's left a legacy of body adornments, legal marijuana, free attitudes about sex, homosexual openness and single parenthood, all of which helped explain the United States today. The shaking continues. We must wonder what kind of legacy we are leaving the next generation.

As the Vietnam War ended, America was again faced with sobering statistics; 58,119 Americans killed in battle, 153,303 wounded, and 1,948 prisoners of war/missing in action. These numbers do not include the many who suffered PTSD and later became deathly ill from exposure to things like Agent Orange. Many more died as a result. This was indeed, sobering information.

Archbishop Jaroshevich, now 84 years old, prayed this would be the end of killing. However, history shows that would not be the case. What was next?

"But the wisdom that is from above is first pure, then peaceable, gentle and willing to yield, full of mercy and good fruits, without partiality and without hypocrisy."

James 3:17 NKJV

"Beware of the leaven of the Pharisees, which is hypocrisy. For there is nothing covered that will not be revealed. Nor hidden that will not be known. Therefore whatever you have spoken in the dark will be heard in the light, and what you have spoken in the ear in inner-rooms, will be proclaimed on the housetops."

Luke 12:1b-3 NKJV

"But seek first the kingdom of God and His righteousness, and all these things shall be added to you."

Matthew 6:33 NKJV

Chapter 15

What Was Next?

Time marched on, and the shaking continued. Many years earlier, after the Jarosheviches were released from the death camp and returned home, he gave a stern warning:

"We came to America, we have learned and talked to two people that know the value that Americans have to appreciate, and that is she and I. You are American people, you are not grateful. No, no, and because you are not grateful to God for America, you go farther from God and continue to go farther from God ... especially things like this, man who believes in God and has the Word of God."[1] It was a stern warning.

In 1981, after an extended illness, Ksenia Jaroshevich went home to be with the Lord. Losing his wife of so many years was hard on Dr. Jaroshevich. He often expressed his grief by writing his lamentations and sharing them with those close to him.

After the loss of his wife, Konstantin Jaroshevich continued to write, knowing he would see her again in heaven.

He remained in their humble home in Virginia Beach, where he continued to write and remain active in his local Church of Christ. Late one evening, in a vain attempt to change a light bulb over his writing desk, Dr. Jaroshevich fell.

It was 1984, and although the bulb did not get changed, he brought a light into the world that would continue to shine for so many. His broken heart was healed as he joined his wife in the presence of the Lord.

As values continued to change, so did society. It seemed the original values of our founders were slowly being eroded away. Was it still "In God We Trust," or was the trust of this nation being placed in man? Our values began to compete with each other. The shift was becoming wider than ever and impacting the daily lives of people.

In his book, *A King Is Coming*, Paul Wilbur explains, "Instead of America the Beautiful, a nation known for our unity and generosity, we have become known as a people who are terribly divided, angry and intolerant of each other. Instead of our great diversity bringing us rich blessings, we have allowed battle lines to form within our nation on any front you may imagine – race, gender, religion, politics, ethics, and economics."

You name it, and there is conflict about it: Political Correctness vs. Biblical Correctness; Religion vs. God. What is your world view?

But what is conflict? Conflict is war! Here we go again. The difference this time is, we are warring with ourselves. It is a war between two world views and the war is now here at home. We live, work, play and worship on the battlefield. History has shown, time and time again, war brings death.

God's standard has been the same, yesterday, today and tomorrow. Our government, entertainers, many educators, and those with power and wealth feel very comfortable opposing and changing the laws of God. There has arisen, a great distrust for our leaders, as their ethical standards appear to be on a downward spiral.

For almost a decade now, our previous administration, and those opposed to God's laws, have begun changing the most powerful and blessed nation on earth into a self-centered, perpetually offended, racially divided, demanding, radically indoctrinated social justice mob, assaulting what is right and defending what is wrong. Why is that? Are they afraid or unable to stand up and fight for what is good and right? Do they not know the difference?

Paul Wilbur declares, "When a nation takes a stand against the clear counsel of God, that nation is just begging to be judged, and eventually it will."

Ask yourself: what would we see if we looked at America through the eyes of God? We would see a nation suffering through the consequences of its man-made, ungodly decisions. We would see our nation going down the road of moral decay. Worse yet, we would see the apathy of those observing the increasing evil in our midst as we continue to walk further away from God.

We would see a nation where violence is becoming normalized and so many are filled with anger and hate. Horrifying cases of child and animal abuse are reported daily. Bullying is terrifying our students, and there does not seem to be much concern for the victim. We would see our young dying due to increasing rates of suicide and drug overdoses. Deaths due to opioids alone doubled between 2015 and 2016. The divorce rate continues to climb as families crumble. We would see a nation at war over words, feelings and values, a war between good and evil.

Alveda King, in her book *America Return to God*, writes, "During the 20th century, the door was opened to invade the wombs of mothers, the stability of the family, the sanctity of marriage, and the sacredness of the human personality. In the name of civil rights, abortion was legalized by the sanction of the *Roe v. Wade* case. Over 55 million babies have been legally aborted in America since then." What about the rights of the unborn?

We would see the greedy striving, by whatever means, to gain money and power, while families are hungry and poorly clothed. We would see a government leading this nation to division instead of unity. We would see some so busy trying to determine what gender they will be for the day, then demanding society cater to their decision. Has political correctness so confused our identity, we would see the raising of a genderless generation? Sadly, you will see young children forced into sexual activities, so the lust of someone's flesh can be satisfied.

We would also see so many bound by the chains of addiction, from alcohol and drugs to pornography and other immoral activities. We would see many impotent churches where man has misinterpreted the Word of God, producing false teachings, leading the sheep astray.

There are churches where Satanism is the foundation. There are many churches where the truth is not spoken for fear of offending someone, yet Jesus offended many. Not speaking the truth, often in itself speaks volumes.

In Charisma Magazine, Todd Starnes quotes, "Silence in the face of evil is itself evil: God will not hold us guiltless. Not to speak is to speak. Not to act is to act."

Have we not heeded the warning of Archbishop Jaroshevich?

The warning so strongly issued by Konstantin Jaroshevich still stands.

What happens when we choose the word of man over the Word of God? What happens when we offend God?

"There is a way that seems right to man, but its end is death."

Proverbs 16: 25 NKJV

"Do not be deceived, God is not mocked; for whatever a man sows, that he will reap."

Galatians 6:7 NKJV

"For those who live according to the flesh set their minds on things of the flesh. But those who live according to the Spirit, the things of the Spirit.
For to be carnally minded is death, to be spiritually minded is life and peace."

Romans 8:5-6 NKJV

"Therefore do not let sin reign in your mortal body, that you should obey it in its lusts."

Romans 6:12 NKJV

Chapter 16

What Happens?

"This day I call heaven and earth as witnesses against you that I have set before you, life and death, blessings and curses. Now choose life, so that you and your descendants may live."

Deuteronomy 30:19 NKJV

What happens when we offend God? What does God say about this? He has plenty to say, but will we listen?

Which will you choose? The way of man or the way of God? The way of man brings curses and death. If we continue on our current path, offending God, we will not only be cursed ourselves, we will pass those curses onto future generations, our children, and their children. Will one generation war against another? God's warning is very clear.

Although many of the curses placed upon us are self-inflicted as a result of sin and poor choices, others may have been passed down through the generations. Either way, there are grave consequences for offending God. These curses destroy people, families, neighborhoods and nations. They are overwhelming forces of destruction, revealing the results of man's fatally limited perspective. They are rooted in evil.

And it is not over. The shaking will continue. It will grow stronger. This will be necessary for God to permanently reestablish His will for the earth. Our nation has suffered an apostolic assassination. The race for faith and the reformation of New Testament Christianity is now on. The war will intensify in heavenly places as we shift back to God's law. God also has plenty to say to those who choose to please Him and follow his law.

In his book, *A King is Coming*, Paul Wilbur sums it up:

"If we live according to God's biblically revealed standard, we receive His favor, protection, grace, provision, and the smile of His presence. Those requiring allegiance to political correctness will undoubtedly resist

us strongly ... but I would ask yet another question of you: is it better to please God or man?"

Which will you choose? What legacy will you leave? It is time to decide.

"But it shall come to pass, if you do not obey the voice of the Lord your God, to observe carefully all his commandments and His statutes which I have commanded you today that all these curses will come upon you and overtake you."

Deuteronomy 28: 15 NKJV

"If you do not carefully observe all the words of this law that are written in this book, that you may fear this glorious and awesome name, THE LORD YOUR GOD, then the LORD will bring upon you, and your descendants extraordinary plagues- great and prolonged plagues-and serious and prolonged sickness."

Deuteronomy 28:58-59 NKJV

"For I, the LORD your God, am a jealous God, visiting the iniquity of the fathers

upon the children to the third and fourth generations of those who hate Me."

Exodus 20:5 NKJV

"See that you don not refuse Him who speaks. For if they did not escape who refused Him who spoke on earth, much more shall we not escape if we turn away from Him who speaks from heaven, whose voice then shook the earth; but now He has promised saying, 'yet once more I shake the earth but also heaven.' Now this yet once more indicates that removal of those things that are being shaken, as of things that are made, that the things that cannot be shaken will remain. Therefore, since we are receiving a kingdom which cannot be shaken, let us have grace, by which we may serve God acceptably with reverence and godly fear."

Hebrews 13:25-28 NKJV

"Now it shall come to pass, if you diligently obey the voice of the LORD your God, to observe carefully all His commandments which I have commanded

you today that the LORD your God will set
you high above all the nations of the earth.
And all these blessings shall come upon
you and overtake you, He is God.

Deuteronomy 28:1-2 NKJV

"Then if my people who are called by My
name, will humble themselves and pray
and seek my face and turn from their
wicked ways, I will hear from heaven and
forgive their sins and restore their land.
My eyes will be open and y ears attentive
to every prayer made in this place."

2 Chronicles 7:14-15 NLT

Chapter 17

It Is Time

It is time to leave a generational impact of blessings, not curses on the world.

It is now time to rebuild, where America has been spiritually and emotionally torn down.

It is time to stop the shift and close the divide.

It is time for a counter-culture that will stand on God's word, not a subculture.

It is time to replace greed and arrogance with humility and authority.

It is time to invade the darkness and spread the light of truth.

It is time for the continuation, not the replacement of God's plan for our lives, our health, peace, joy and freedom.

Consecrated

It is time to make a difference, as the silent majority did, by no longer being silent during the 2016 election.

It is a time to be heard loud and clear.

It is time to recognize the unfolding battle plans between the kingdoms of good and evil.

It is time to take our place as the watchmen on the wall.

It is time to claim our heavenly inheritance and live in the fullness of it.

It is for a time such as this, one must decide to either live in the glory of God or a man-made hell on earth.

It is time we consecrate our children to the LORD.

It is time for the real church to wake up; they do not have to remain powerless.

It is time for churches to do an honest self-evaluation---What kind of church are you?

Are you preaching the Word of God or adhering to the word of man?

Are you herding sheep or loving them and feeding them?

Are you looking for those who are lost or are you too busy with programs, budgets or technology?

Are you just too busy?

Has your church been infiltrated by Satanism or the Jezebel spirit?

Are you ready for spiritual warfare, including deliverance?

Does your church recognize the spiritual gifts and anointings sitting in your church each week?

Does your church permit those gifts to operate or are they confined to a religious box?

Does your church operate in an atmosphere of mediocrity and settling for just getting by?

Is your church a place of entertainment, spiritual malaise and declining membership?

Has the worship in your church moved to such an anointed level that the flood gates of heaven open?

Does the Holy Spirit have free rein to take over your services and produce a move of God, bringing conviction and a truly intimate relationship with God?

Are healings, miracles, signs and wonders occurring in your church?

Is your church moving forward in advancing the kingdom of God and exposing the Antichrist system?

The shaking is getting strong

As spiritual warfare continues to intensify and confronts the church, there is encouragement to pastoral leadership to provide assurance to persecuted Christians. The Lord clearly sends His message to the seven churches, loveless, persecuted, compromising, corrupt, dead, faithful and lukewarm (Revelation 1-4).

To the faithful Church, He says:

"Because you have kept my command to persevere, I will keep you from the hour of trial which shall come upon the whole world, to test those who dwell on the earth."

Revelation 3:10 NKJV

In His message, the individual members of the churches are urged to hear what the Holy Spirit says. His is a message of prophecy and awaits a response. The Holy Spirit is saying "come." He is calling the churches and the bride of Christ to invite those outside to enter in. He is working through the church and its members to bring those in darkness into the light, before it is too late. He will empower those who witness and patiently endure. He is calling. Will you accept His invitation? Will you listen?

But wait! Off in the distance...do you hear it?

Chapter 18

Listen

*"Surely it will be well with your
remnant; Surely, I will cause the enemy to
intercede with you in the time of adversity
and in the time of affliction."*

Jeremiah 15:11 NKJV

I hear voices. They are being raised in every sector
of society.

I hear students defending their faith throughout
America's schools. I hear parents objecting to the anti-
Christian teachings in our schools. I hear workers in
government and public offices refusing to perform duties
that go against their values. I hear people from all walks

of life boldly defending their right to pray, carry a bible and honor this nation's flag.

I hear intercessors and prayer warriors praying with new found authority, joining together and standing in the gap for our churches and our country. I hear them drowning out the voices of evil with the voice of truth. I hear these voices saying "it is time." Everywhere, groups are gathering with a quiet urgency. The numbers are growing, as their prayers and worship are reaching the heavens, and God is listening. He is preparing to respond.

But, there is more! From all over, God is calling back the remnant, and they are coming by the thousands.

A battle like no other is brewing. The whole earth is shaking. The explosion is coming. It will be the final battle before all things are restored and the new church will be aligned with the plan of God. Which side will you be on? The warnings of the Old Testament prophets are coming to life daily. The words of Dr. Jaroshevich are ringing loud and clear.

As the antichrist system and all the darkness with it emerges, the persecuted church and the body of Christ are being called to the final war. Christians must learn how to fight this battle. We know the physical enemy; we can see it and touch it. The spiritual enemy can no longer hide, as the strategy of the enemy is revealed.

The Army of God is rising up. It will not be an easy battle. Two kingdoms will clash violently, yet God promises to protect those who believe in Him.

As we accept, not fear, His supernatural power, God will give us our battle assignments and position us accordingly. We will be shifted into many new places as we enter that realm.

Through Him, we will transition from war to triumph. Our great inheritance will be preserved and no one will take our crowns.

Are you still listening? It is in the distance, coming closer, getting louder. I hear trumpets. I hear the approaching thunder of hoof beats. I see the four horsemen riding in our direction. They ride with a warning, a message, and an opportunity, and we must listen carefully.

The arrival of the four horsemen and their message should not be a surprise. They bring confirmation of the end times message Jesus gave his disciples in Matthew 24 and 25 and Revelation 6:1-8. It is a message of what must and will take place. It will be a time of tribulation.

The first horse is the white horse. It, and its rider represents the one who deceives. Jesus warns us to resist alluring deception and He will return to pass judgment on those who follow thee false prophets and false Christ.

The red horse comes representing war. By removing peace, there will be much shedding of blood, as people slay one another, as nation rises against nation and Kingdom rises against Kingdom. The red horse will make way for the black horse, and riding together, they will bring hunger and disease.

Finally, the pale horse and its rider, followed by Hades, will bring pestilence and death. They have the authority over a fourth of the earth, to kill with sword, famine, pestilence and the wild beasts of the earth.

This is the very powerful message of what is to come. It is a message of warning to the disobedient. It is a message of judgement. God's message is the same yesterday, today and tomorrow and because His judgement is conditional, it is also a message of hope.

The message also presents an opportunity to take advantage of His unconditional love. It is an opportunity to be transformed, before it is too late. It is an opportunity to reach out to a hurting world and join Him in this final battle to save this world from total destruction. It is an opportunity to consecrate our children and grandchildren to God.

The Lord of Lords, the King of Kings, is coming back, in victory, to claim His church. Are you ready? If you have any doubts, I urge you to pray the following prayer out loud.

Dear Heavenly Father;

I know I am a sinner and I ask you for your forgiveness. I believe you died on the cross, for my sins and rose again. I turn from my sins. I repent for my sins. I invite you into my heart and my life. I want to trust and follow you. I ask these things in Jesus' name. Amen

> *"Let no one deceive you by any means; for that Day will not come unless the falling away comes first, and the man of sin is revealed, the son of perdition, who opposes and exalts himself above all that is called God or worshiped, so that he sits as God, showing himself to be God.'*

2 Thessalonians 2:3-4 NKJV

> *"And then the lawless one will be revealed, whom the Lord will consume with the breath of His mouth and destroy the brightness of His coming. The coming of the lawless one is according to the working of Satan, with all the power, signs and lying wonders."*

2 Thessalonians 2:8-9 NKJV

> *"You shall seek them and not find them- Those who contend with you. Those who war against you shall be as nothing. As a nonexistent thing'*

For I, the LORD your God, will hold your right hand, saying to you, Fear not, I will help you."

Isaiah 41:12-13 NKJV

Chapter 19

A Final Thought

"Remember those who rule over you, who have spoken the word of God to you, whose faith follow, considering the outcome of their conduct."

Hebrews 13:7 NKJV

This book has been written, not only to pay tribute to the life of Konstantin Jaroshevich but to ensure his legacy continues to bring wisdom, inspiration, hope, faith, and encouragement to future generations.

His is a story of a young immigrant arriving in New York City in 1910 in search of truth and freedom from religious persecution. As he listened to a preacher on the streets of New Yok, the Lord called him for service and he responded.

Consecrated

And so, began a ministry that would take him across the United States, Europe, and to his homeland of Poland. It would be the ministry of a humble man of God who would lead many thousands to the Lord.

Dr. Jaroshevich was ordained a minister when he first completed doctorate degrees in Divinity, Literature and Philosophy. He was unanimously elected as a life President of the Union of Churches of Christ and later ordained as an Archbishop.

Although he was offered the position of Polish Ambassador to the United States, he respectfully declined, knowing such a responsibility would interfere with his work for the Lord. In Poland, he was decorated twice, first by the "Golden Cross" and second by the highest order Poland could give, the cross with the "Polona Virtuty Restitut."[1]

It is the story of a man, whose intense love for people and faith in God, led him on a journey through joy and sorrow, peace, and war, as he impacted many people, towns, countries, and nations along the way.

It is also a historical story of good and evil. It is a story of what we do to ourselves when we stray from the Lord. It is a reminder of the spiritual revival of the 1940s and 1950s, when we were one nation under God, and how the blessings of those days became less frequent as we moved away from His Word. It is an opportunity for us to pause and look within.

This book is to acknowledge the spiritual legacy, more precious than gold, he left to his grandchildren and the blessings he left to all who knew him. What legacy will you leave?

"One generation shall praise your works
to another, and shall declare
Your mighty acts."

Psalm 145:4 NKJV

Finally, it is to honor the mighty God we serve, through whom all things are possible.

I remain eternally grateful that in 1941, my grandfather lifted me from my cradle and **Consecrated** me to the Lord.

About the Author

DR. ALIX JAROSHEVICH WALSH

Dr. Walsh has a Master of Science in Healthcare Administration from Central Michigan University. Upon retiring in 2002, she answered the call to continue her education, obtaining her Doctorate in Ministry along with her ministry ordination. She is now on the faculty of Coral Ridge Seminary in Jacksonville, Florida.

Over the last seven years, Dr. Walsh has served as a prayer minister at Christian Healing Ministries, which practices and teaches healing prayer.

Dr. Walsh resides in Orange Park, Florida with her husband Bob.

You can contact Dr. Walsh at dralixjwalsh@gmail.com.

End Notes

Chapter 1

1. Jones, Robert H, "Blue and White; Dedicated to God." Echos from the Hill, volume 111 #5, May 1980

Chapter 2

1. Jones, Robert H, "Blue and White; Dedicated to God." Echos from the Hill, volume 111 #5, May 1980
2. Jaroshevich, Konstantin," I Should Be the Faithful Servant of God." Personal letters and writings.
3. Kolodziej, Wladyslaw, "A Personal Historical Sketch," Brest-Litovsk, November 11, 1939
4. ibid

Chapter 3

1. Jones, Robert H, "Blue and White"; Dedicated to God." Echos from the Hill, volume 111 #5, May 1980
2. Klodziej, Wladyslaw, "A Personal Historical Sketch," Brest-Litovsk, November 11, 1939
3. Jaroshevich, Konstantin, "I Should be the Faithful Servant of God." Personal letters and writings.
4. Jones, Robert H, "Blue and White"; Dedicated to God." Echos from the Hill, volume 111 #5, May 1980
5. ibid

Chapter 4

1. Klodziej, Wladyslaw, "A Personal Historical Sketch," Brest-Litovsk, November 11, 1939
2. ibid
3. ibid
4. ibid

Chapter 5

1. Bajko, Paul, "The History of the Churches of Christ I Poland." Polish Christian Ministries, Bel Air, Maryland 2001; Co published by Wydawnictwo, Slowo i Zycie, Warszawa, Poland
2. Kolodziej, Wladyslaw, "A Personal Historical Sketch," Brest-Litovsk, November 11, 1939
3. Bajko, Paul, "The History of the Churches of Christ I Poland." Polish Christian Ministries, Bel Air, Maryland 2001; Co published by Wydawnictwo, Slowo i Zycie, Warszawa, Poland
4. Kolodziej, Wladyslaw, "A Personal Historical Sketch," Brest-Litovsk, November 11, 1939
5. Jaroshevich, Konstantin, "I Should Be the Faithful Servant of God" personal letters and writings.
6. Jones, Robert H, "Blue and White; Dedicated to God." Echos from the Hill, volume 111 #5, May 1980
7. ibid
8. Bajko, Paul, "The History of the Churches of Christ I Poland." Polish Christian Ministries, Bel

Air, Maryland 2001; Co published by Wydawnictwo, Slowo i Zycie, Warszawa, Poland
9. Kolodziej, Wladyslaw, "A Personal Historical Sketch," Brest-Litovsk, November 11, 1939
10. ibid
11. ibid

Chapter 6

1. www.Britannicia Online Encyclopedia, WW1 and WW11
2. Runbeck, Margaret Lee, "The Great Answer," Chapter 18, 1944 The Riverside Press, Cambridge, Massachusetts.
3. ibid
4. Jones, Robert H., "Blue and White; Dedicated to God." Echos from the Hill, volume 111 #5, May 1980
5. Runbeck, Margaret Lee, "The Great Answer," Chapter 18, 1944 The Riverside Press, Cambridge, Massachusetts.
6. ibid
7. ibid
8. ibid
9. ibid
10. Jones, Robert H, "Blue and White; Dedicated to God." Echos from the Hill, volume 111 #5, May 1980
11. ibid

Chapter 7

1. Bajko, Paul, "The History of the Churches of Christ in Poland." Polish Christian Ministries, Bel Air, Maryland, 2001, Co-published by Wydawnictwo, Slowo i Zycie, Warszawa, Poland
2. ibid
3. Jones, Bob, "History of the Polish Church" interview with Konstantin Jaroshevich
4. ibid
5. ibid
6. ibid
7. ibid
8. ibid
9. ibid
10. ibid
11. Jones, Robert H. "Blue and White; Dedicated to God." Echos from the Hill, volume 111 #5, May 1980
12. 12 Jones, Bob, "History of the Polish Church" interview with Konstantin Jaroshevich
13. Jones, Robert H. "Blue and White; Dedicated to God." Echos from the Hill, volume 111 #5, May 1980

Chapter 8

1. www.Britannicia Online Encyclopedia, WW1 and WW11
2. Webster's Ninth New Collegiate Dictionary, 1989

3. Jaroshevich, Konstantin, "From the Baltic Sea on the North to the Black Sea on the South-It Calls for a Helping Hand." Article in an unknown publication.
4. www.Britannicia Online Encyclopedia, WW1 and WW11
5. www.National WW22 Museum.org.
6. ibid
7. www. Presidency uscb.edu Franklin D. Roosevelt. D Day prayer
8. ibid

Chapter 9

1. Webster's Ninth New Collegiate Dictionary, 1989
2. Bajko, Paul, "The History of the Churches of Christ in Poland," Polish Christian Ministries, Bel Air, Maryland, 2001, Co-published by Wydawnictwo, Slowo I Zycie, Warszawa, Poland
3. ibid
4. ibid
5. ibid
6. Kennedy, O.S.B., Bishop Brian J. "Apostolic Succession of Bishop Brian J Kennedy, O.S.B., April 25, 2001, www. Celticorthodoxchurch.com
7. Webb, Henry E, "Disciplina-History of te Churches of Christ in Poland." Fall 1992, Volume 52, No.3.
8. ibid
9. ibid
10. ibid

Chapter 10

1. Bajenski, Andrzej and Karel, Pitor, "Horizons, Celebrating the 90th Anniversary of the Polish Churches of Christ." June-July 201
2. Taken from personal correspondence.
3. "Standing Episcopal Conference of Orthodox Bishops." www.ukranianorthodoxchurchworldwide.com
4. ibid
5. Webb, Henry E, "Disciplina-History of the Churches of Christ in Poland." Fall 1992. Volume 52, No. 3.

Chapter 11

1. "Royal Office to Crown o Belarus and Prince of San Luigi" www.san-luigichurch.org
2. "Standing Episcopal Conference of Orthodox Bishops."
3. www.ukranianorthodoxchurchworldwide.com
4. ibid
5. Orthodox Catholic Church in North America. www.oratory.tripod.com
6. ibid
7. "Royal Office to Crown o Belarus and Prince of San Luigi" www.san-luigichurch.org
8. ibid
9. "Standing Episcopal Conference of Orthodox Bishops."
10. www.ukranianorthodoxchurchworldwide.com

11.www.independentsacramentalmovement/zhurawersky

Chapter 12

1. "Standing Episcopal Conference of Orthodox Bishops."
   www.ukranianorthodoxchurchworldwide.com
2. ibid
3. "The Apostolic Succession of Most Rev. Richard A. Kalbfleisch, OCF, though the Old Catholic Church of Utrecht, Independent Catholic Church of Brazil and Russian Orthodox Church."
   www.stfrancisocc.org/Succession
4. Tucker, Carol, "The 1950's-Powerful Years for Religion" www.usc.edu
5. "The Revival of Domesticity and Religion."
   www.boundless.com/u-s-history
6. Tucker, Carol, "The 1950's-Powerful Years for Religion" www.usc.e
7. ibid

Chapter 13

1. Tucker, Carol, "The 1950's-Powerful Years for Religion." www.usc.edu
2. ibid
3. ibid

Chapter 15

1. Jones, Bob, "History of the Polish Church". Interview with Konstantin Jaroshevich

Chapter 19

1. Kolodziej, Wladyslaw, "A Personal Historical Sketch. Brest-Litovsk. November 11, 1939

CPSIA information can be obtained
at www.ICGtesting.com
Printed in the USA
FFOW04n1805080518
46534375-48502FF